PUBLISHED BY SOUTHBANK PUBLISHING,
21 GREAT ORMOND STREET,
LONDON WC1N 3JB
WWW.SOUTHBANKPUBLISHING.COM

FIRST PUBLISHED BY EAST STREET PUBLICATIONS, AUSTRALIA

© DAVE EVANS 2008

THE RIGHT OF DAVID EVANS TO BE IDENTIFIED AS THE AUTHOR OF THIS WORK HAS BEEN ASSERTED IN ACCORDANCE WITH THE COPYRIGHT, DESIGNS AND PATENTS ACT 1988.

ALL RIGHTS RESERVED. NO PART OF THIS BOOK MAY BE REPRODUCED, STORED IN OR INTRODUCED INTO A RETRIEVAL SYSTEM, OR TRANSMITTED, IN ANY FORM OR BY ANY MEANS (ELECTRONIC, MECHANICAL, PHOTOCOPYING, RECORDING OR OTHERWISE) WITHOUT THE WRITTEN PERMISSION OF THE PUBLISHERS.

ANY PERSON WHO DOES ANY UNAUTHORISED ACT IN RELATION TO THIS PUBLICATION MAY BE LIABLE TO CRIMINAL PROSECUTION AND CIVIL CLAIMS FOR DAMAGES.

A CIP CATALOGUE RECORD FOR THIS BOOK IS AVAILABLE FROM THE BRITISH LIBRARY.

ISBN 978-1-904915-28-7

BOOK DESIGN BY ALEXANDER BIANCHINI-KOMETER
COVER DESIGN BY GEORGE LEWIS
COVER IMAGE - TIDE CHANDELIER - WWW.STUARTHAYGARTH.COM
BACK COVER - TRANSGLASS BY TORD BOONTJE - WWW.DEDECEPLUS.COM
PRINTED AND BOUND BY DAMI EDITORIAL & PRINTING SERVICES CO. LTD

COOL / KUL / *ADJECTIVE* NEITHER WARM NOR VERY COLD. CALMLY AUDACIOUS OR IMPUDENT. *COLLOQUIAL* SMART; UP TO DATE; SOPHISTICATED AND STYLISH

GREEN / GRIN / *ADJECTIVE* OF THE COLOUR OF GROWING FOLIAGE, BETWEEN YELLOW AND BLUE IN THE SPECTRUM

STUFF / STUF / *NOUN* THINGS OR BELONGINGS NOT NEEDING TO BE SPECIFIED

COOL GREEN STUFF / *ADJECTIVE* PRODUCTS THAT MAKE THE WORLD A CLEANER, GREENER AND, MORE BEAUTIFUL PLACE

cool hunting green

DAVE EVANS

www.southbankpublishing.com

FASHION
jewelry | clothes | bags

beach necklace

A brightly colored necklace made from bits of plastic the artist becky crawford collected on her local beach.

tupperware necklace

A necklace made from recycled Tupperware™ lids which were cut up, fused together then strung with sterling silver.

www.lianakabel.com

extra & ordinary necklace

A necklace made from old rubber bands woven together using the simple but beautiful 'loop-in-loop' technique popular with gold and silversmiths since about 3000BC.

www.mindwhatyouwear.com

eco band

Made from recycled candy wrappers, it's the official wristband of the ecoist website and they plant a tree for every band sold.

www.ecoist.com

rubber bangle

These little red dots were punched out of a piece of rubber to make a hole in another product. Salvaged and repurposed they make a pretty bracelet.

www.lianakabel.com

giggles bracelet

Margaux Lange transforms discarded barbie dolls into unique, handmade art jewelry. instead of being accessorized, ironically, Barbie® has become the accessory.

love letters "I heart U" bracelet

The web is full of listings for companies who are willing to recycle your old computer equipment. Who knows, your old keyboard could eventually reappear as a bracelet like this one. Designer Rebecca Ward says it's perfect for geeks in love!

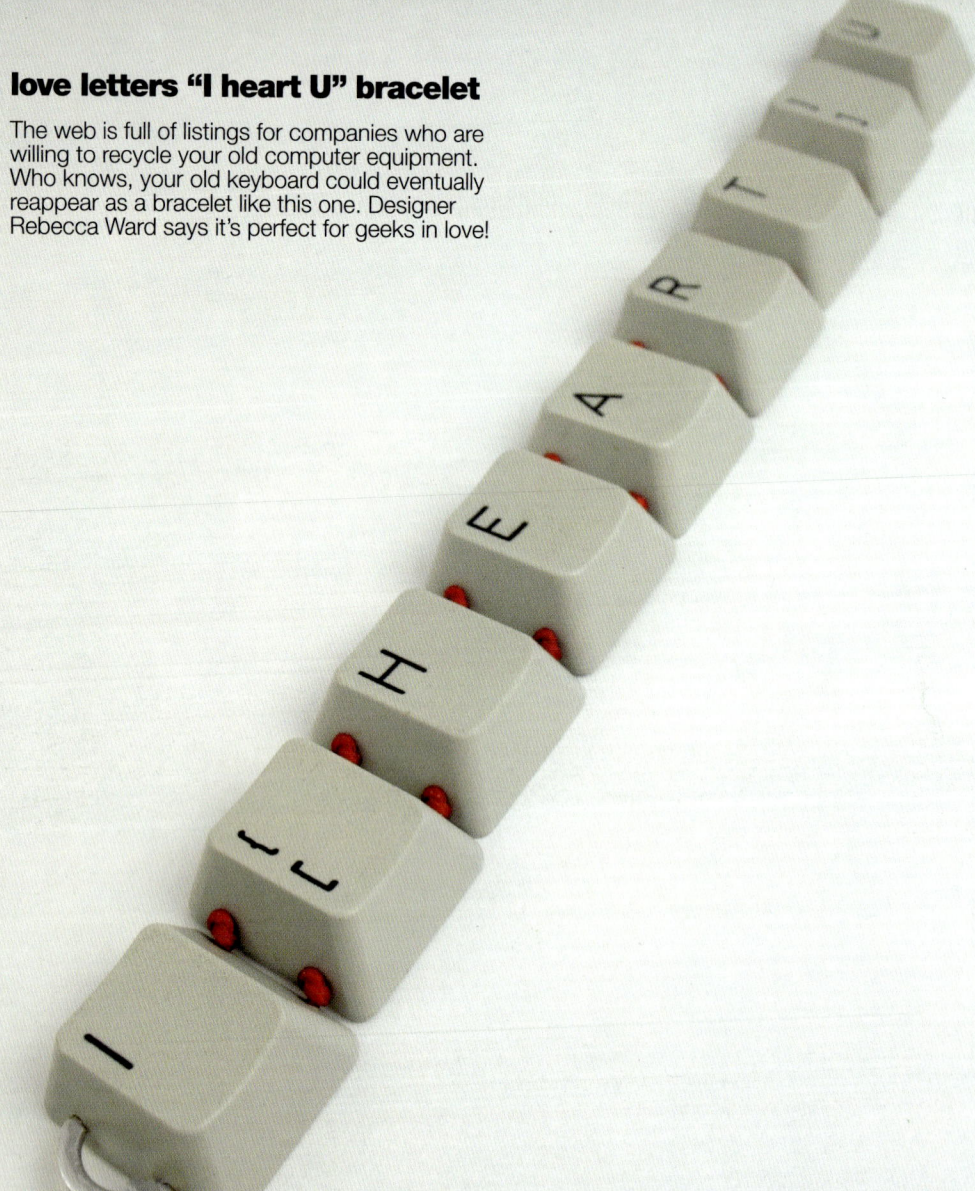

www.rebeccawardjewellery.com

bullet cartridge cuff

Bullet casings collected from a shooting range, garnet beads and a silver clasp combine to create awareness of the transience of life. Some shooters do recycle the casings but many are wasted.

handy bracelet

Made from used mobile phone keypad buttons. The name "handy" refers to the European name for a mobile phone.

knit wit chunky bangle

A bangle fashioned by hand from an old knitting needle.

www.lianakabel.com

like road kill, in a resurrection worthy of the Six Million Dollar Man, have found new life as wrist bands that bear new Japanese movement watch faces.

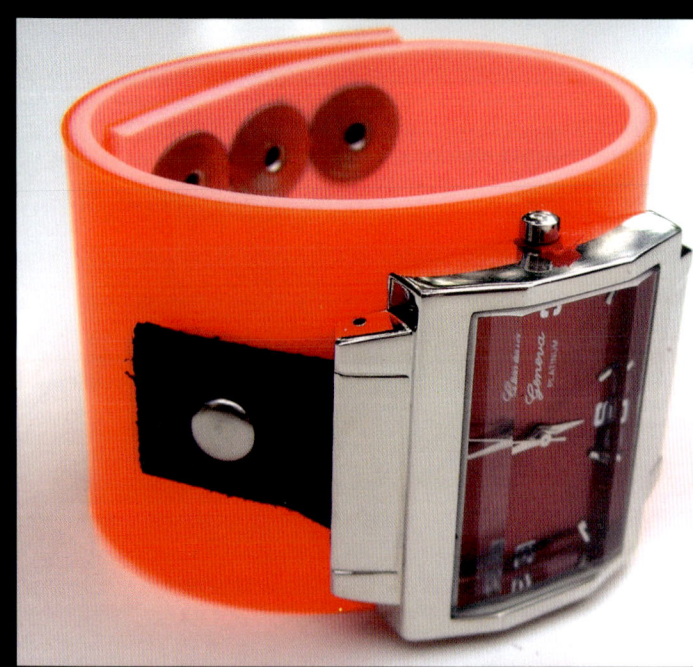

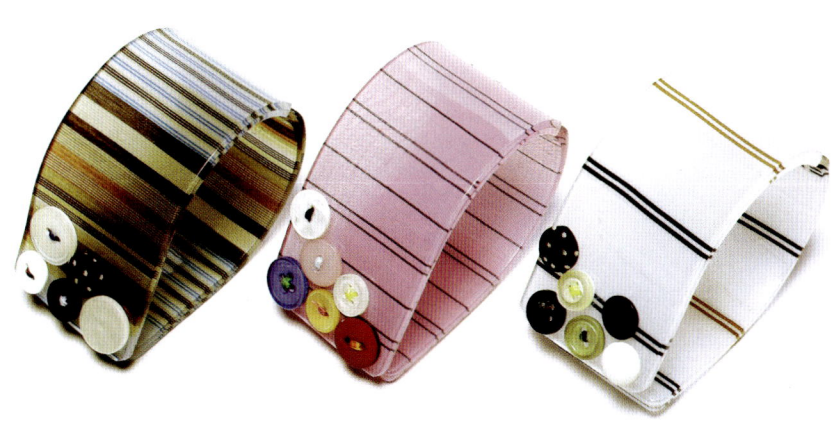

beer and soda can rings

Made of sterling silver and real beer and soda cans, the aluminum is secured to the jewelry with sterling rivets and protected from damage by overhanging ledges.

www.elsewares.com

pinwheel vintage shoe ring

Vintage Barbie® doll shoes were used to create these whimsical rings of sterling silver and plastic. Margaux Lange's jewelry celebrates the contrast and contradiction of mass-produced items transformed into unique, wearable pieces of art.

www.margauxlange.com

knit wit earrings

Vintage knitting needles cut up and reassembled as earrings.

www.lianakabel.com

star pop earrings

Old tins with an enamelled surface are cleaned, cut up and used to create one-of-a-kind designs

love letter earrings

Made from old computer keyboards, the addition of embroidered hearts comments on modern courtship practices; where we once exchanged handwritten love letters, we now rely on chat rooms, text messaging and other online forms of communication.

flower earrings

Sweet little earrings made from recycled plastics and vintage sequins. Designer Liana Kabel says, "if it looks like a lolly, I like it."

www.lianakabel.com

paper beads

Make your own jewelry with these beads. Each one is hand rolled from strips of magazine and catalog pages.

www.junkmailgems.com

nana 100%

Made from old copies of Nana Mouskouri vinyl records, milk bottle tops, pen parts and brass wire, these brooches celebrate the amazing career of the bespectacled Greek diva and come in limited edition releases of 12, each one named after one of the 12 memorable tracks on the album. The patterns are derived from heat pressing the vinyl into heritage textured glass salvaged from old buildings.

www.rebeccawardjewellery.com

birdie brooches

Pretty brooches made from used candy wrappers that would otherwise have been thrown in the trash.

www.tamsinhowells.com

measure up brooch

An old tape measure has been hand folded into a floral brooch with a button center. A handmade steel pin back allows you to attach it to your clothing or wherever else you wish.

www.lianakabel.com

rosette

This pretty pink rosette is a brooch in the shape of a flower made from vintage kimono and obi silk material.

www.pomme.com.au

hair control system

Old keyboards and new elastic
combine to create hair elastics
that control wayward hair styles.

www.rebeccawardjewellery.com

Extremely cute flower rosettes made with reclaimed cashmere and a vintage bead center.

global warmers

Organic cotton underwear screen printed with thermo chromic ink. When the underwear warms up the sea overcomes the land, communicating the effects of global warming.

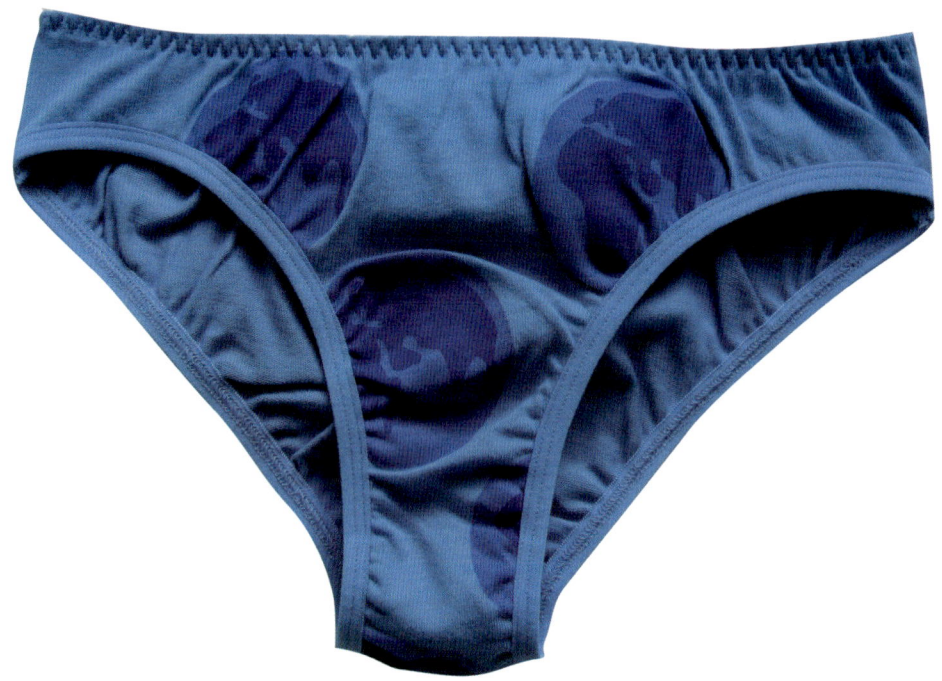

www.greenknickers.org

stop deforestation

Silky underwear that are 60% hemp and 40% silk. The bikini line is printed with the words "stop deforestation".

www.greenknickers.org

the womble

These 99% recycled trainers are made from a broad range of recycled products including ex-military parachutes and jackets, jeans and old t-shirts. The footbed is made from recycled foam.

www.terraplana.com

organic cotton sneaker

Designed by John Patrick these sneakers are made from organic cotton. To be considered organic the product must not use synthetic pesticides, herbicides, fungicides, fertilizers or antibiotics in the production process.

www.johnpatrickorganic.com

car sandal

These 99% recycled sandals are made from the interior of old cars and include pieces of seat belt and leather seats. The sole is made from old car tires.

www.terraplana.com

juniper quilt

Made from recycled Pakistani quilts, this shoe uses minimal glue and vegetable dye. The fact that it is lightweight means it takes less energy to transport it to you when you purchase it online.

www.terraplana.com

souls massage thongs

These comfy slides mould to the shape of your feet with wear and the bubbles give you a therapeutic massage as you walk. Made from non-toxic rubber using 25% recycled content, they are 100% recyclable.

www.souls-australia.com.au

melissa slides

Brazilian company Melissa uses a patented recycled and low toxic plastic product called "mel-flex" to create these shoes. It has no toxic smell and lessens the tendency for feet to sweat. 99% of their industrial residues are recycled and they melt down their left-overs to make more shoes!

sk8 belt buckle

This belt buckle was created from an old skate board and, as such, is a unique and functional piece of art honoring the original board designer and the person who had the fun of riding it. Designer Becky Hickey says "from an artistic standpoint, I love board graphics, and when I was younger I'd spend hours at my local shop admiring every detail of artwork on the newest shipment of decks."

www.beckycity.com

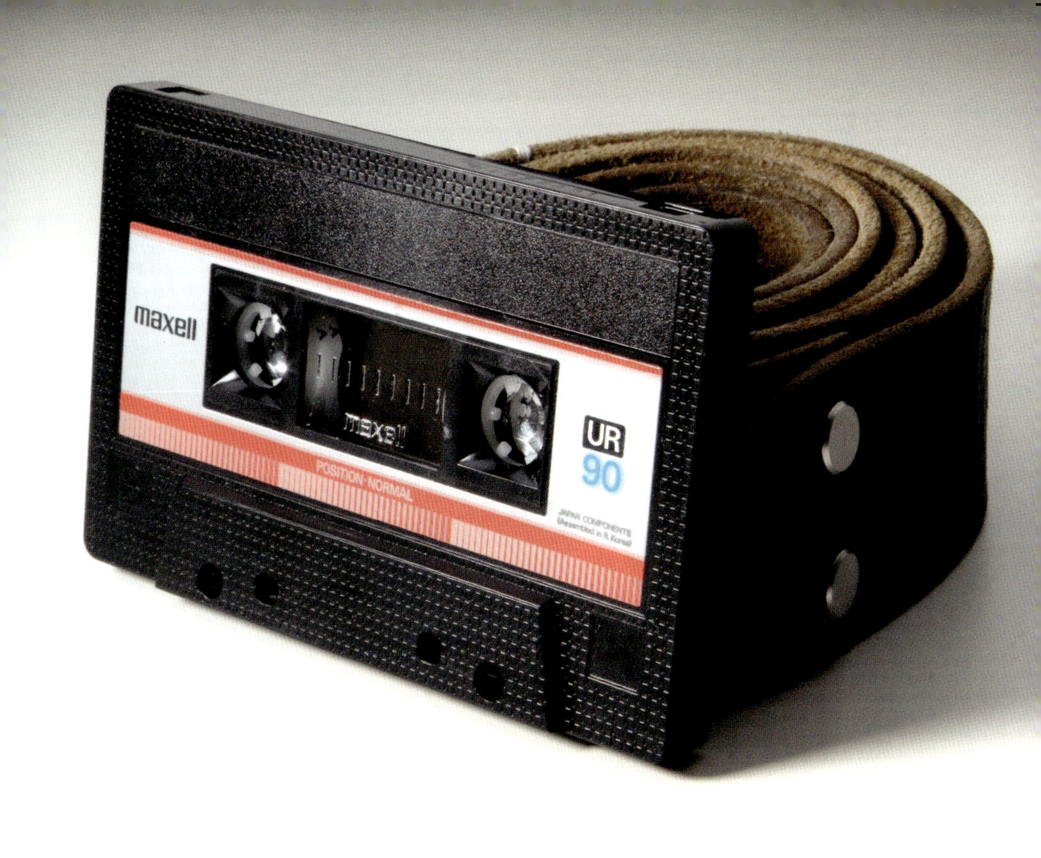
maxell
maxell
UR
90
POSITION·NORMAL

cross country

Indigenous has provided organic and fair trade quality apparel since 1984. This garment is 45% environmentally friendly tencel, 35% alpaca and 20% merino wool, allowing exceptional airflow to naturally regulate body temperature.

www.indigenousdesigns.com

bamboo jeans

Made from 50% bamboo, 48% organic cotton and 2% lycra silk trim these jeans are both stylish and comfortable. Designer Carol Young creates pieces that are functional and seasonless, and will live a long lifetime in your wardrobe. Carol donates 1% of revenue to "1% for the Planet" and donates surplus fabric to local children's arts programs for non-profits and schools.

www.undesigned.com

DIY umbrella skirt

Why not turn an old umbrella into a waterproof skirt? All you need is fabric from an unwanted umbrella, elastic and a zipper. Replayground is where discarded materials take on a new life!

www.replayground.com

sad earth organic tee

This original artwork by Ksubi also appears on posters and stickers. They're all designed to create awareness and assist in the fight against global warming.

www.ksubi.com

tupperware dress

A one-off design made from recycled Tupperware.™

www.lianakabel.com

plasticoat

Made from used plastic bags fused together by a hot iron and quilted onto a blanket from a dumpster. Handmade one-of-a-kind clothing by Tammy Lyons.

www.thimblescratch.com

S!X dress

When designers Sprynskyj and Boyd started out, money for fabrics was limited, so the duo began taking existing garments apart and using the material to create patterns. This led them to adopt those "deconstructed" prototypes, promoting them to the status of garment. S!X successfully disrupts the design process to create "recycled" pieces that maintain a strong sense of tailoring.

www.freestyledesign.info/31-s!x.html

seed polka range

Hand printed using water-based dyes, Bird is an exquisite range of luxury eco clothing manufactured using solar power. They were Australia's first climate neutral fashion brand.

www.birdtextile.com

amy dress

Ciel uses a wide range of organic linen, cotton, bamboo and hemp/silk crepe blends. Their prints are phthalate and azo free. In addition to intelligent eco-design and socially conscious production methods, Ciel recommends low wash temperatures to reduce energy emissions and the "slow fashion" concept of timeless modern design that you can build on each season. Ciel was among the first carbon neutral UK fashion companies offsetting their carbon footprint by partnering with www.staro.org (Save The Amazon Rainforest Organization).

bolivian knits

Bolivia is the poorest country in South America, but the 25 women who knitted these naturally dyed, organic alpaca woolen garments work in self-managed groups and receive a "fair" wage for their work, along with health and dental care and schooling for their children.

www.oeufnyc.com

safety

Design cooperative, SECCO, links innovative designers, producers, material collectors and recyclers into a growing international and professional network of people united by a spirit of innovation, quality and sustainability. Designer Päivi Niemi has created this bag from used seatbelts.

www.seccoshop.com

rub-a-dub

Designer Miia Kylmänen created this briefcase from a used car tire inner tube.

www.seccoshop.com

on the road

Made from a car tire inner tube,
this large toiletry bag can be taken
on the road next time you go away.

www.seccoshop.com

the jimi

You might find the odd tiny speck in these beautiful translucent wallets, but that's because the people at jimi are committed to using post industrial waste – polypropylene and polycarbonate – in their construction. More than that, they also donate 1% of their sales revenue to the environment through the "1% for the Planet" initiative.

www.thejimi.com

billbag

Second time around (or 2xO) are committed to creating quality, functional street wear from long lasting products such as billboards, fire hoses, car seatbelts and tire inner tubes. The billboard cut to create this bag originally served to advertise the first Shrek movie.

www.2xo.com.au

prophyla-p-tics

Hip laptop sleeves cut from used PVC vinyl advertising billboards are a great way to protect the Apple of your eye. No two are ever the same.

www.haul.com.au

sk8bag

This is a one-of-a-kind hand crafted tote bag made by Becky Hickey from a retired skateboard (originally designed by Shepard Fairey). Although she washes the decks and removes the grip tape, Beck says, "I don't add anything… I'm simply reusing something that was already there."

www.beckycity.com

plastic tote bag

This tote is made by Brazilian company Melissa who use a patented environmentally sensitive recycled plastic called "mel-flex".

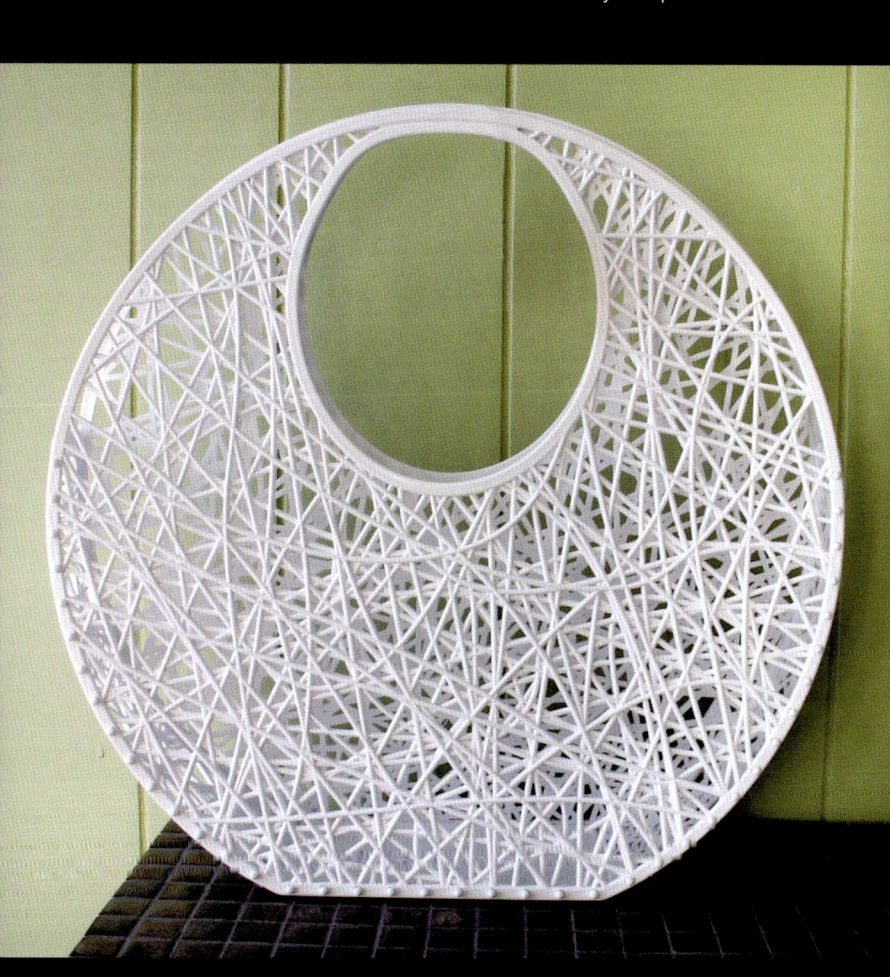

masha

Elegant and funky, the masha is a chic metallic shoulder bag with an eco twist. It's hand made in Brazil by the As Panteras do Lacre cooperative. There's over 1600 recycled aluminum can tabs crocheted into each bag.

www.dedeceplus.com

key bag

A stunning bag created from used computer key boards and lined with long-lasting nylon.

www.joaosabino.com

just beg

Naulila luis is a designer from the Designwise Collective in Portugal, where designers are united by a desire to create pieces that "tell a story." This bag's story is about second chances; it's made from recycled felt tip markers and constructed by workers at the drug-free unit of the Tires detention facility (Lisbon).

www.experimentadesign.pt/designwise

the everything / anything bag

The people at ecoist are keeping tons of trash out of landfills (they repurpose misprinted and discontinued candy wrappers) to bring you these purses that are handmade, sturdy and waterproof.

www.ecoist.com

cardcase

A unique laptop case made from discarded cardboard. It's designed to act as a protective sleeve for the computer with cardboard indenting to take the force of a blow. The cases can be personalized with your own initial.

www.farmdesigns.co.uk

bamboo purse

A compact little purse made from the world's fastest growing woody plant.

www.shopregeneration.com

suitcase

A striking bag
made from recycled
suit jackets.

www.suitcase-london.com

If you're going for a more formal look at work – throw your tie over your shoulder. Vintage men's ties make a colorful bag for work and play.

www.shopregeneration.com

UM

Josh Jakus's tactile bags resemble pebbles washed up on a beach. They're made from industrial waste felt.

www.joshjakus.com

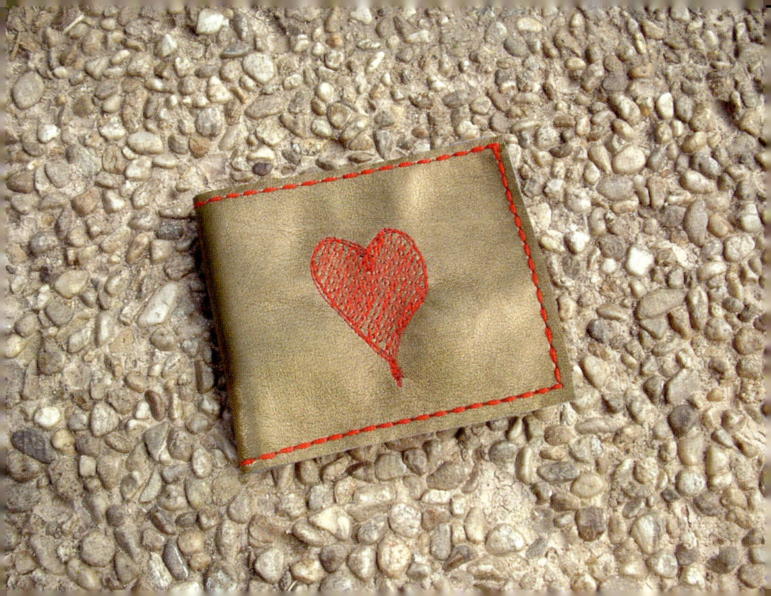

zipper mini purse

The zipper mini purse is made by a women's cooperative in the Philippines from used aluminium juice containers, mostly collected by school children as an after school job. They're very durable and the aluminum lining provides thermal protection.

www.bazurashop.com

paper bag

Billboard paper is a strong, durable, semi-impermeable material which is especially difficult to recycle due to the high ink content. However, designer Jos van de Meulen gives them new functionality by folding them double-thick and sewing them with rough thread into large bags, ideally suited as laundry baskets.

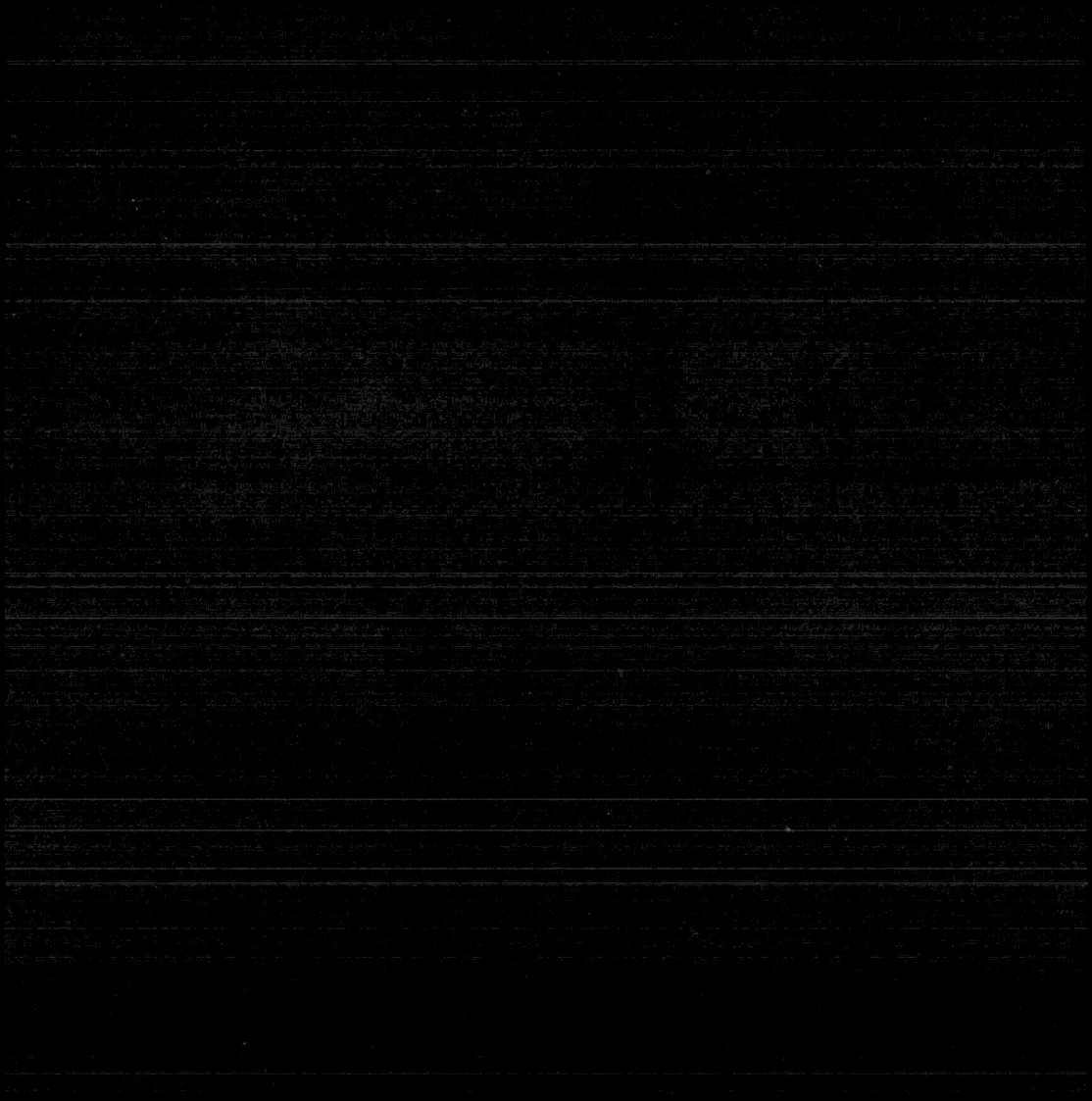

STUFF

gadgets | electronics | stationery

kahana solar waterproof bag

With the kahana pack you've got no more worries about getting any of your valuables wet. This is the first totally waterproof solar bag on the planet, allowing you to keep your portable electronics dry while still being connected to the sun via an integrated solar panel - no matter where you are.

www.clearbluehawaii.com

blue sun solar backpack

The perfect backpack for the go-anywhere-anytime traveler. The blue sun backpack integrates a flexible, weatherproof solar panel into a uniquely designed bag module. The bag module attaches to an adjustable, ergonomic sub-frame support system for maximum comfort and support.

www.clearbluehawaii.com

mana solar claw

Solar technology in a universal sleeve and accessory compartment. No matter what your taste in backpacks might be, mana claw is the perfect solution for anyone looking for portable power. Just attach and go.

www.clearbluehawaii.com

sun trap handbag

Powered by a flexible solar panel on the outside of the bag, the sun trap bag has an electroluminescent interior light that comes on automatically as you unzip the bag. If you accidentally leave the bag open, the light will automatically turn off after 15 seconds to conserve power.

www.rosannakilfedder.com

solar charger

Charge cell phones, mp3 players, pda's and more with nothing but sunlight. Solar style puts the power of the sun in the palm of your hand.

www.solarstyle.com

solio charger

A portable, renewable power source that draws energy from sunlight, storing it in an internal battery and using it to charge virtually all mobile electronic devices.

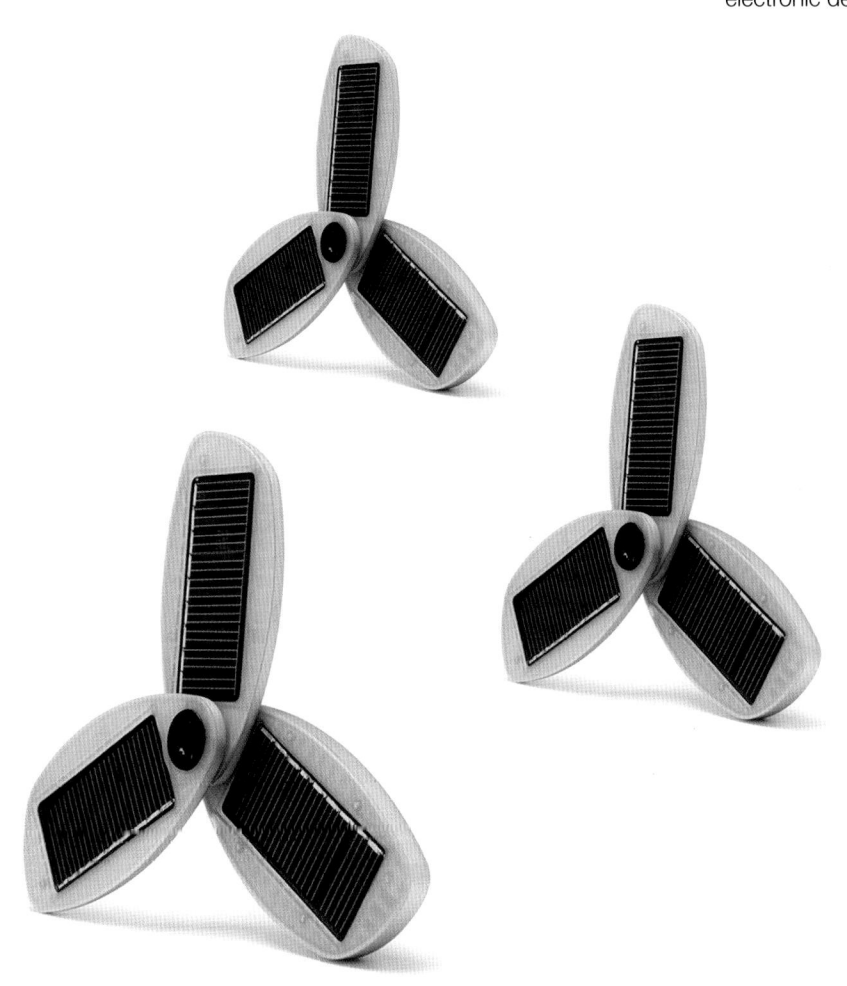

www.todae.com.au

helicopter with solar blades

These lovely wooden helicopters with revolving rotor blades make a fun and educational present for a vehicle-obsessed child. The rotor blades go round in the sunshine and stop when in the shade – a great demonstration of solar power in action.

www.nigelsecostore.com

wind-up charger

A great backup for when your phone is running out of power. It's small and light enough to fit comfortably into most bags and comes with a number of different adaptors included for popular makes of phone. Ideal if you are going camping or if you are away from a main power source.

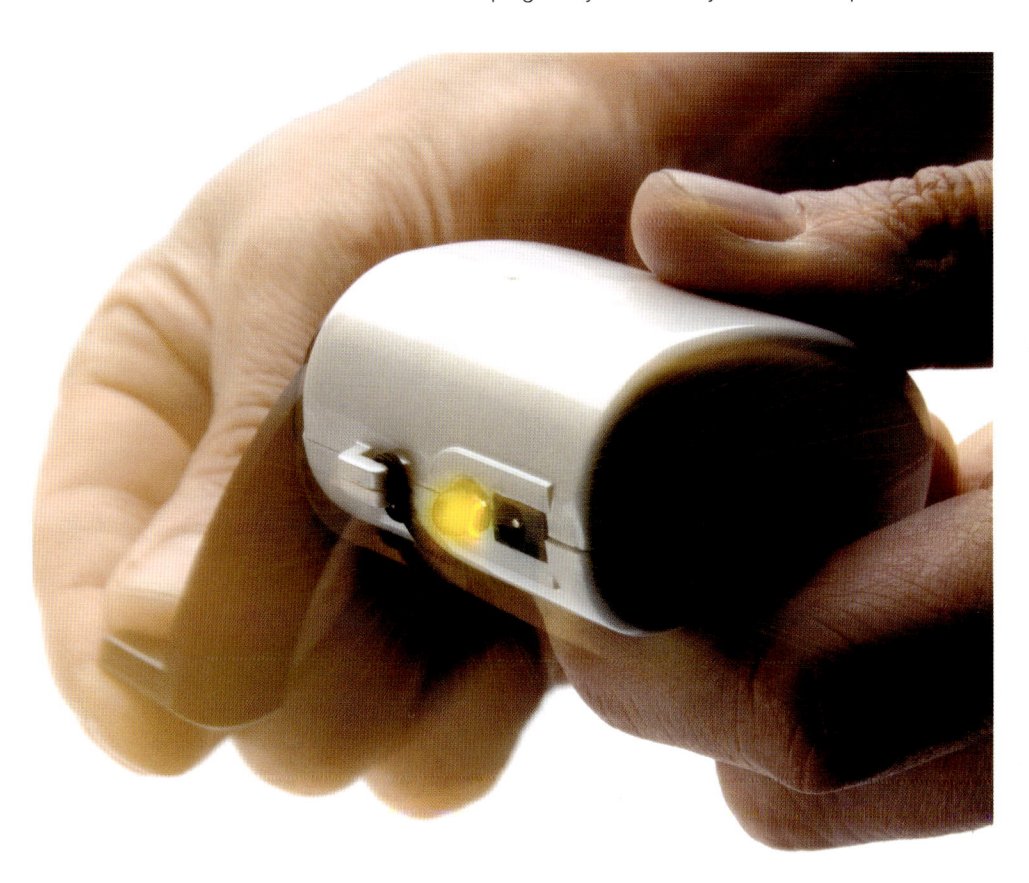

www.porta-charge.co.uk

indigo lantern

A self-sufficient wind-up LED
lantern. No batteries required.

www.freeplayenergy.com

squeezy torch

A funky torch powered by built in rechargeable batteries. There's an efficient mechanism in the handle that converts mechanical energy to electricity.

www.neco.com.au

wattson

A stylish home energy monitor, wattson shows you exactly how much power you're consuming in your home at any given time. Turn any household appliance on, off or to standby and you'll see exactly what difference it makes to your energy consumption. You can link wattson to your computer and download chronologically stored energy data for the previous year to see if your efforts at minimizing consumption have worked. You can also join wattson's online community to see the difference you're making as a group.

half a teaspoon showerwatch

Helps you keep track of your time in the shower and, as a result, become more aware of your water use. It's all part of the half a teaspoon® awareness program – to visualize the world's available water and use it more consciously.

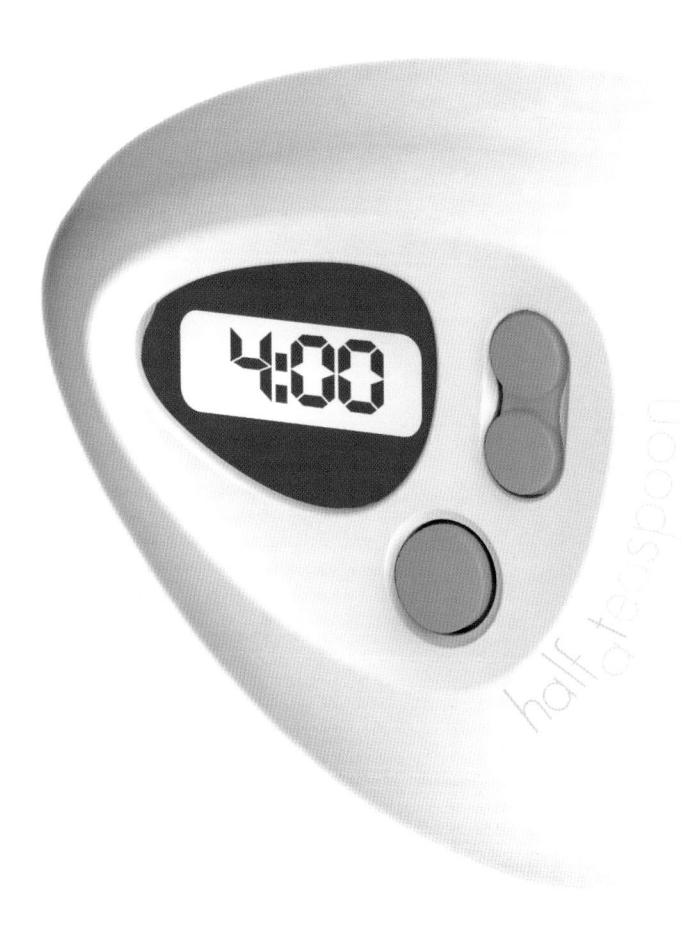

www.halfateaspoon.com

bamboo tft monitor and mouse

Just one of the reasons bamboo is such an eco-friendly woody plant is that it can be harvested in 3-5 years versus 10-20 years for most softwoods. Make the most of it with this computer monitor and mouse, which incorporate bamboo in the casing.

www.nigelsecostore.com

jimi iPod nano case

It looks fine and translucent, but this 100% recycled, 100% recyclable polycarbonate case is made from the same stuff used to make cash registers and bullet-proof glass.

www.thejimi.com

mskyo – mama said knock you out

These speakers take us back to the days of the old ghetto blaster by making stylish use of granny trolleys. They're equipped for cd, radio and ipod.

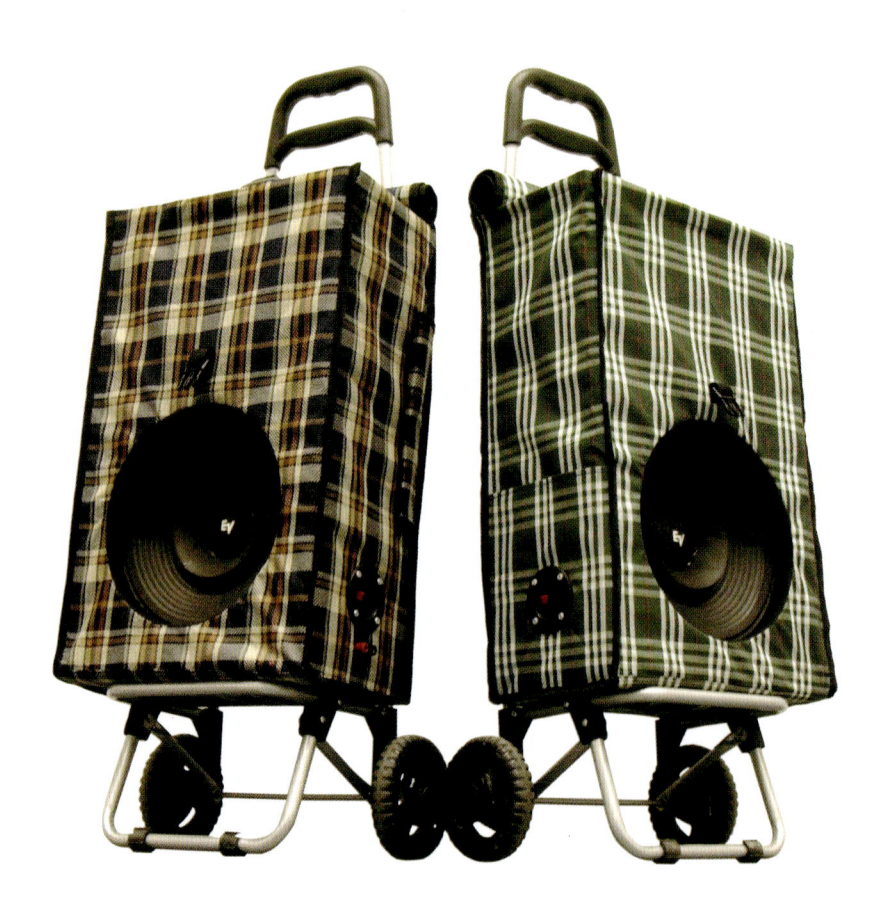

www.claassen-partner.de

air pod

Breathe easy with this personal air purifier that is so compact you can take it with you wherever you go. Just plug it in and create your own clean air zone.

www.blueairstore.com

j-card luggage tag

Make a statement with luggage tags made from the j-cards of old cassette tapes.

www.honorable-mention.com

A cd stand from aki kotkas made from old vinyl lp's. Be reminded of the good old days when you used to put the needle on it.

motherboard notebook

Eye-catching notebooks covered in computer motherboards rescued from landfills.

www.shopregeneration.com

license plate journal

Made from used license plates and rubber inner tubes, these journals still carry the occasional nick and mark from their days on the open road.

www.haul.com.au

elephant poo poo paper

100% recycled and odorless products from elephant poo! They collect dried elephant dung from conservation parks and rinse it with water, retaining just the fibrous materials from the grasses, bamboo and fruits the elephants have eaten. It's then boiled and combined with additional fiber from banana trees and pineapples to create a paste which is spread thinly over a mesh-bottomed tray and dried in the sun.

www.poopoopaper.com

otsu planners

Weekly and monthly planners made from 100% post-consumer recycled paper and soy-based inks. Don't waste a day, just fill in your own dates so you can start using them any time of the year.

green map

Get a green-eyed view of New York city with this map that charts the city's wealth of ecological resources and community spirit. Created with special help from the New York City Environmental Fund and Greenacre Foundation.

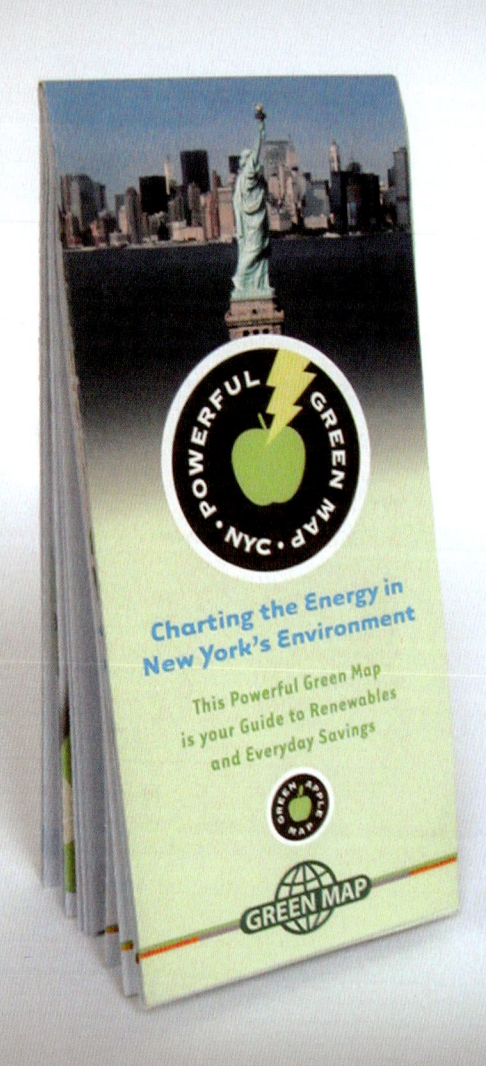

www.greenapplemap.org

christmas tree poster

Use a little bit of paper but save a whole tree. Pin your pixilated tree to the wall and decorate it, knowing it will stay green for many christmas celebrations and won't drop needles on the floor.

www.atypyk.com

eco

A waste paper bin entirely handcrafted from reused paper. Each model is unique and made in Switzerland.

www.366cm.com

paperbox

Unused billboard paper from test prints has been folded double-thick and rough sewn to create this rectangular box. It's ideal for storing newspapers until they make it to the recycling depot themselves.

www.dedeceplus.com

change the world 9 to 5

A great book from the makers of *Change the World for a Fiver*, bringing you another 50 everyday actions that you can do during your working day to make the world a greener place.

www.the-green-apple.co.uk

this into that

This book kit contains 15 do-it-yourself recycling projects using discarded plastic.

www.replayground.com

crude

Exquisitely packaged and branded, a limited edition 50ml "parfum" of real crude oil makes an ironic statement, fortelling the future of one of the 20th century's most influential raw materials.

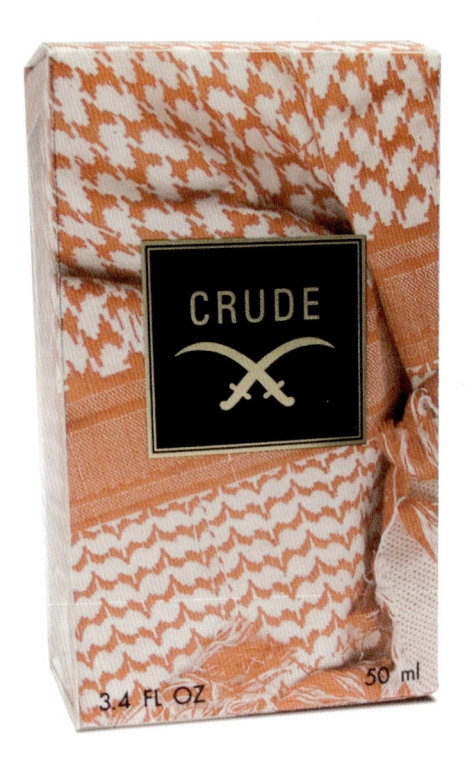

3.4 FL OZ 50 ml

www.citizen-citizen.com

hand grenade oil lamp

From actual US Army surplus grenades, these lamps are available in their natural color, or gilded in either gold or silver. This piece is a sure fire ice breaker when entertaining guests.

www.elsewares.com

desk pendulum clock

This innovative clock features a bicycle chain ring and recycled tire rubber face which appears to float in mid-air.

www.resourcerevival.com

With an old stove burner cover for a face, this clock uses the function keys from a retired pc keyboard to show the time.

HOUSE
décor | kitchen | sculpture | lighting | comfort

This creation addresses a much overlooked topic of interior design – the washing. It's a drying system that utilizes the central heating system of your house.

ivy

Made from recycled plastics and resembling a climbing plant, this is an unusual yet attractive way in which to hang your clothes.

www.ivy.mos-office.net

buckle up key holder

An ingenious wall mounted key holder from buckle up designs made from a seatbelt buckle, each one rescued from a used car.

www.nigelsecostore.com

hook

366cm is the name of Swiss designers Sergio Streun and Vincent Schertenleib. Here they've found a new use for an old phone card.

www.366cm.com

zilka

A sixties-inspired digitally printed hanger made from sundela board, which is produced from recycled and compressed newspapers.

grapple

Made from bio-resin and cotton, this hook is an adaption of well used products from a construction site into a functional product for the home.

www.ryanfrank.net

pinch

Artist Jos van der Meulen discovered that clothes pegs grow on trees. In secret forests he harvests the wood and transforms them into unique little statues.

www.dedeceplus.com

noming vase

Frank Kerdil's vase is inexpensive and almost impossible to break. It's made from a unique paper-based material, which is 51% chalk. You can write or draw on them (but they're 100% waterproof) and use them over and over again, so by buying them you'll be doing your grandkids, not to mention the planet in general, a big favor.

www.yousaytomayto.com

wooden seed boxes

Jouko Kärkkäinen is a Finnish industrial designer and artist who loves to work in wood and values trees enormously. These innovative little wooden seed boxes each contain a seed, making a stylish little gift that encourages the propagation of more trees.

www.ply.fi

ecoforms

Made from renewable grain husks, ecoforms are a long lasting alternative to plastic. These plant pots look great and are suitable for inside and outside use.

www.ecoforms.com

tab 'b'

Smoking pollutes the atmosphere and plants clean it. This creation combines an ashtray with a plant pot in order to neutralize the effect of smoking in a visual, environmental and aromatic sense.

www.vitaminliving.com

x-tray

A set of 5 ceramic pots, which can be configured in several ways. Great for growing a range of herbs, plants or health-giving wheatgrass.

www.vitaminliving.com

transglass

By Toord Boontje, a collection of glassware made from recycled wine and beer bottles, demonstrating hard, sharp, clean forms and original bottle colors.

www.dedeceplus.com

6 pack

Who would have thought a 6-pack would be useful on more than one level? The fun people at atypyk show us how.

www.atypyk.com

P.E.T abuse

"Chalices" made from old PET plastic bottles for that special impromptu party.

www.redstr.com

organik glass series

Made of boiled scraps of glass with a drilled and hand polished base

A glass-made heart composed of the upper parts of two bottles. Creator Antonio Cos explains that the bottle keeps its expressive and geometrical characteristics, but it acquires a new poetic dimension.

3 in 2

When we don't have a rolling pin at home we generally use a bottle, so why not make the role official?

www.antoniocos.com

solar cooker

This nifty little cooker reflects the sun's rays onto mirrored cone-shaped panels, concentrating the energy on a central axis. Food can be kept warm within it at temperatures of around 195°F/90°C.

www.bcksolar.com.ar

Cork is an efficient insulating material and works well in this trivet created from used wine corks and recycled glass beads

bike chain bottle opener

A new spin on the classic bottle opener. It's got a flexible, repurposed bike chain handle with a beautiful anodized aluminum head.

www.resourcerevival.com

cutting up knives

These beauties form part of a limited production run of bottle openers crafted from old knives. The creators say, "the future of mass production is mass customization".

www.pervisioni.it

candy wrapper placemat

All ecoist products are made from recycled, organic or earth-friendly materials, and they're manufactured through ecoist's network of fair trade partnerships around the world. These have been woven from silver candy wrappers, and food and drink spills wipe off easily.

www.ecoist.com

bottled spice

Joao Sabino is a designer from Portugal. He's created these salt and pepper containers from old bottles and cork.

candy wrapper coasters

Made from faulty or discontinued lines of candy wrappers, these coasters merge design with social and environmental consciousness to provide stylish, functional and durable products that people love to own.

www.ecoist.com

motherboard coasters

We don't normally recommend you put your coffee anywhere near your computer's motherboard, but in this case, retired motherboards become the perfect place to rest your mug.

jar tops

With a set of these screw-on plastic tops, you can turn your old jars into vessels with a purpose.

www.jorrevanast.com

long flat b pack

This new invention has all the benefits of a twist top bottle in a convenient, environmentally friendly pak. A lifecycle inventory study confirmed that the use of the b-pak produces lower environmental burdens than a glass wine bottle.

www.cheviotbridge.com.au

eco kettle

The innovative eco kettle has a unique double chamber that encourages you to measure out exactly how much water you want to boil on each occasion. It'll save you electricity, water, money and time, making it better for the planet, too.

www.nigelsecostore.com

aerogarden

The aerogarden employs "aeroponic" technology, which suspends plant roots in a 100% humid, oxygen rich environment. Insert pre-seeded grow pods, add water and nutrients, plug it in and watch your plants grow rapidly with 100% germination guaranteed. Harvest your fresh fruit and vegetables for up to six months from a single planting without waste or pesticides.

www.aerogrow.com

log bowls

The log bowl harkens back to traditional lathed wooden bowls, typical of beginner woodworking. Made from log off-cuts, each one contains naturally occurring imperfections.

www.loyalloot.com

Folds flat for storage then unfurls to hold coins, keys, fruit and other small treasures. This bowl is made from grey industrial wool felt considered excess by the factory that was discarding it.

catchall basket

Made from used potato chip bags collected on the streets of nepal. The bags are cleaned and wrapped around dried grasses to create these one-of-a-kind baskets.

fabulous bowl

Designer Carlos Montana has a "life-oriented" design philosophy, whereby he seeks to create a long-term positive social, economical and cultural impact through his creations. The fabulous bowl is made from can tabs which he collected himself and is particularly interesting because of its structure and diverse functions. When open it makes a small container for fruits or candy and seems to "float" on the table. When closed and upside down (as in the photo) it is an object of strange beauty and maybe even a receptacle for objects such as pens and pencils.

www.carlosmontana.com

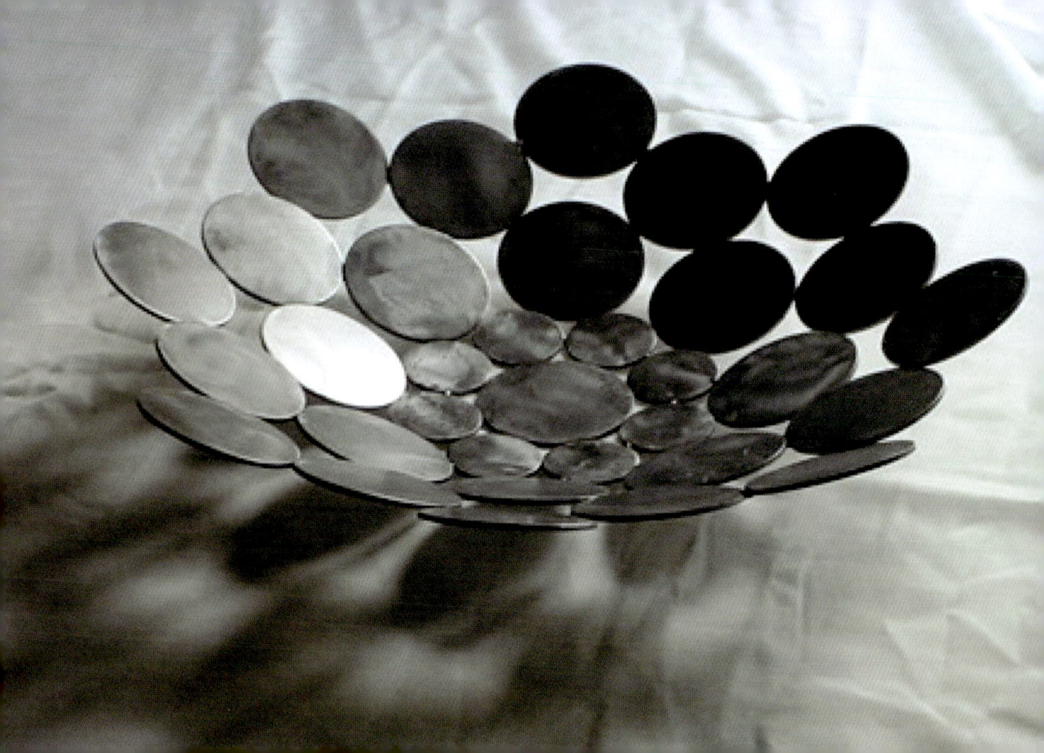

war bowl

Toy soldiers from the Battle of Waterloo are melted together to form a decorative bowl representing something of a paradox – a reminder of happy childhood games on the one hand and a representation of war and all its horrors on the other.

www.thorstenvanelten.com

vintage record snack bowl

Made from classic vinyl lp's, these bowls are 100% recycled and 100% cool. When you place your order, you can choose which genre you'd like (but not which particular artist).

www.elsewares.com

fruit bowl

19 old bottles are cleaned, cut at a specific angle and joined to create a bowl suitable for fruit or just to look at.

www.joaosabino.com

trashforma 05

Trashformaciones is an artists' collective creating installations from recycled objects, like this larger than life sculpture in the form of flowers made from stainless steel tubing and repurposed old drain holes.

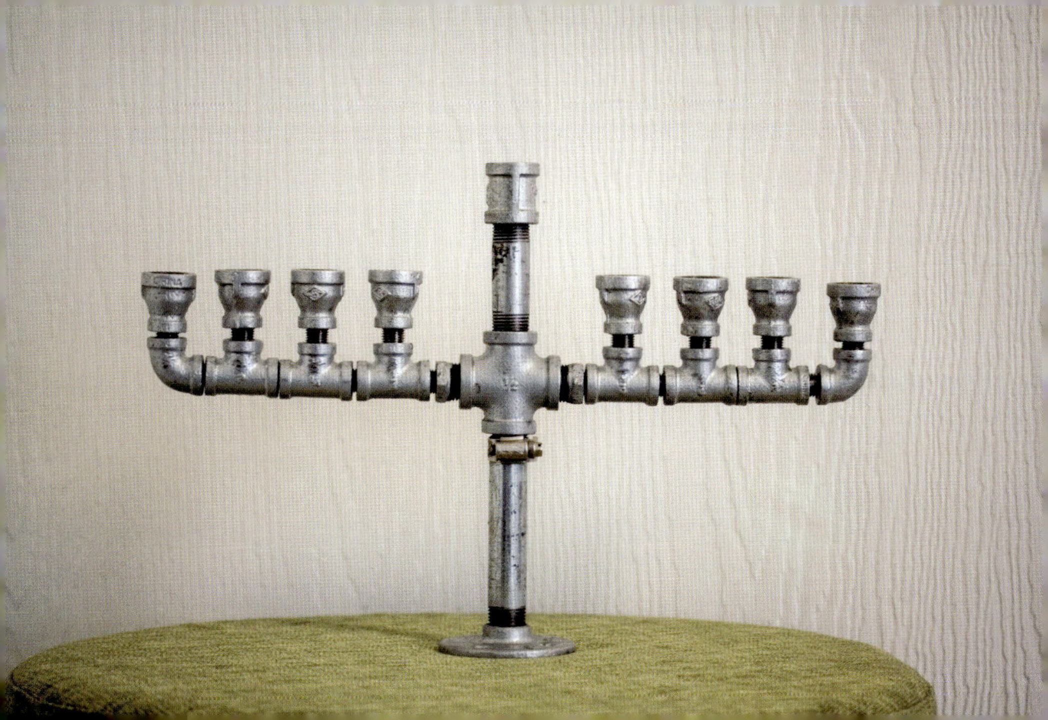

tornado

Made entirely from recycled materials
(mostly old vacuum cleaner parts)
and brought to life with the imagination
and skill of cutting edge designer, Ptolemy.

www.hubcapcreatures.com

usually on the side of the road, and therefore bear the scars of their previous lives in the form of scratches and abrasions, which add texture and history to the creatures.

rooster and owl

One-of-a-kind avian sculptures built from many different cans and tins, mostly salvaged from the trash.

www.annabuilt.com

kingfisher

Ptolemy, the creator of hubcap creatures, has also taken on the challenge of using discarded shopping trolleys for his fantastic creations.

www.hubcapcreatures.com

trashforma 04

This installation is a 3.5m cube made by the union of 166 used stainless steel sinks. It acts as a solar filter, projecting light rays through the sink holes into the interior of the cube to stunning effect.

www.trashformaciones.com

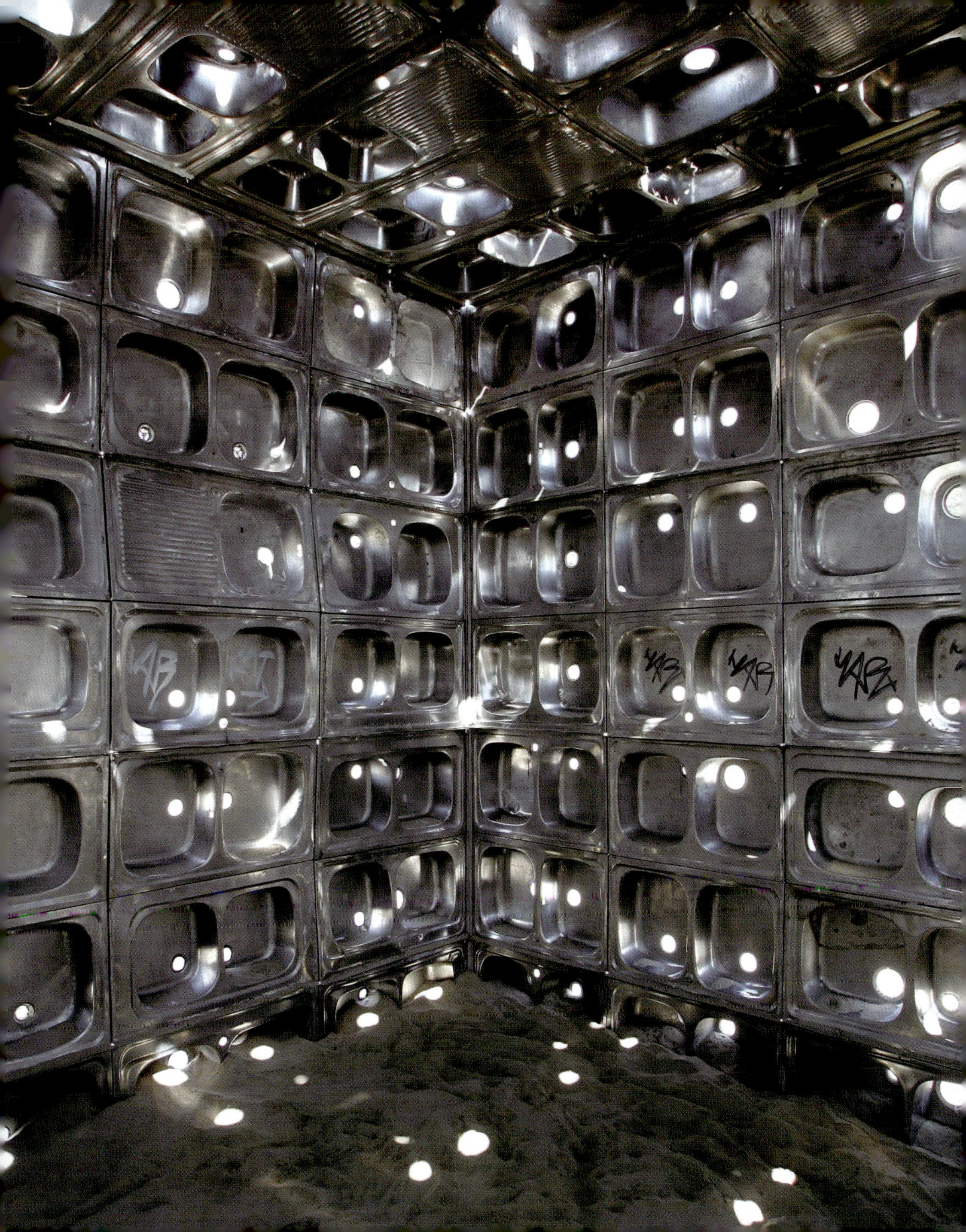

happy blackout

An ironic little candle that reminds us we don't have to burn carbon to create light. Simply light a tea candle, place it in the happy blackout stand and place an old burnt out light bulb in front of it. They look great and make a fun conversation piece when 4 or 5 of them are lined up along a wall.

www.stiletto.de

glow brick

OK, it's not a replacement for the national grid, but it does make a great night light, and with little or no electricity required, it's environmentally friendly. Simply charge the glow brick in sunlight or under lights, take it into a dark room and leave it glowing in the darkness – it'll work for up to about 3 hours.

www.nigelsecostore.com

helene

Make using less electricity sexy with this simple little shade. Place a tea candle in a wine glass, light it and then wrap this little lampshade around the glass – viola!

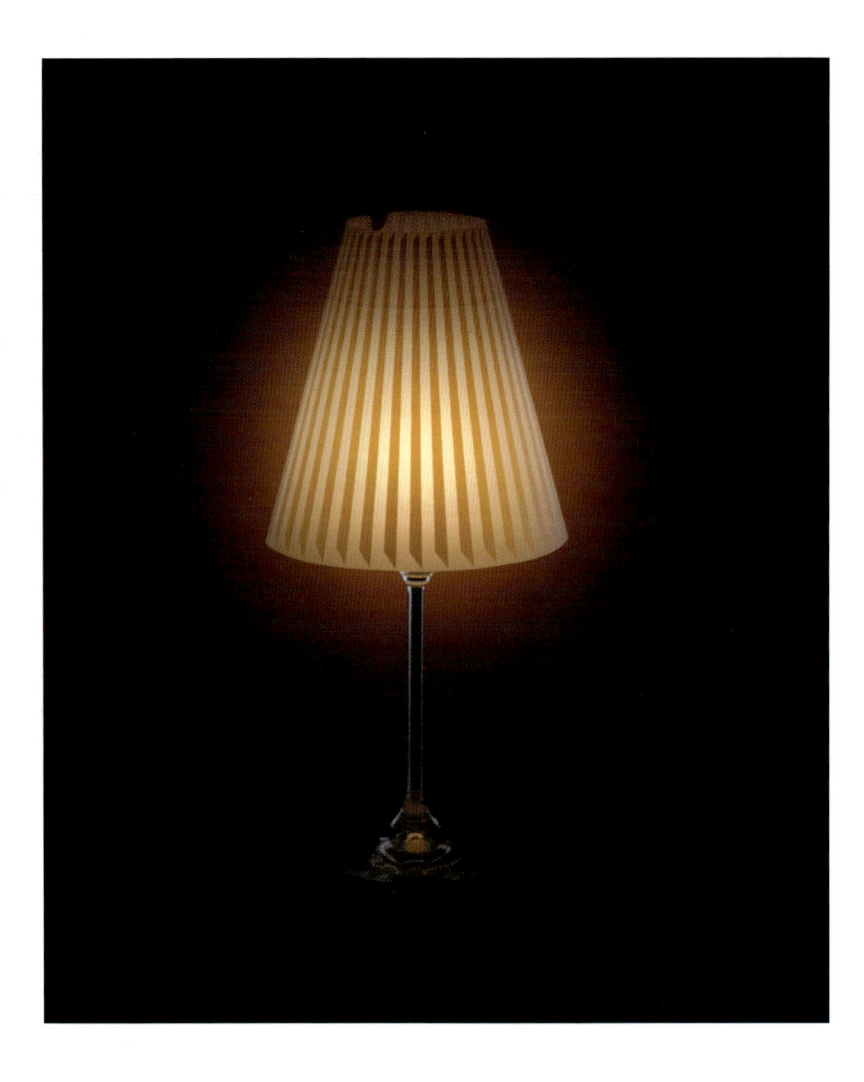

www.pa-design.com

flamp

A blackout at a design exhibition inspired designer Marti Guixe to create this phosphorescent lamp for the next exhibition. Phosphorescence is a process in which energy absorbed by a substance is released relatively slowly in the form of light.

www.guixe.com

flute light

It's just a light bulb and some repurposed cardboard, but when environmentally aware designer Giles Miller brings them together, they're something really special.

www.farmdesigns.co.uk

ruminant bloom

Ruminant bloom are beautiful, blossom-like lamps that are made from preserved sheep stomachs, all natural and perfectly unique.

www.julialohmann.co.uk

the laundry lamp ($250k) series

Detergent bottles reclaimed from London streets become functional lamps using shrink wrapped low energy compact fluorescent tubes. Industrial designer Julian Lwin, who has worked on the design of such bottles, knows it takes about $50k in research, design and development to get a new laundry product to market, so he decided to name his repurposed bottles after the $250k in investment the 5 bottles represent.

lightboots

Vintage boots have been carefully selected and either hand painted, customized or unzipped to reveal the light of the energy-saving light bulbs installed within.

www.claassen-partner.de

igloo

Made from polystyrene and an energy saving
light bulb, the igloo transforms common packing
material into a precious light envelope.

www.antoniocos.com

hand light

A highly original lighting creation made from bits of an old leaf blower and a ceiling light fitment found in a dustbin.

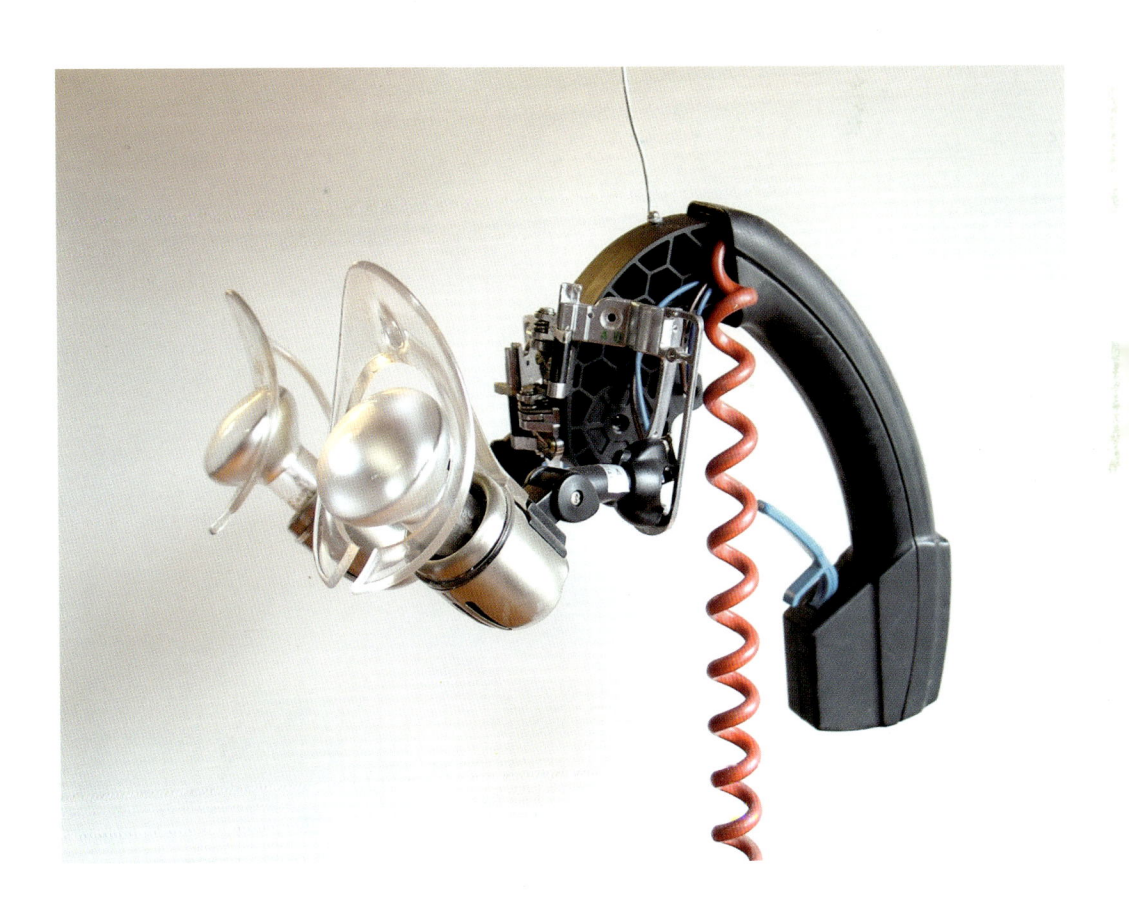

www.hubcapcreatures.com

Polyurethane products are everywhere. It's in the foam in your chair, the grip on your tennis racquet, your surfboard, car seat and even under your mouse pad. Little wonder we have so much of it going to landfills when those products are out of use. Artecnica found a new use for recycled polyurethane when they "scribbled" the design for this pendant light.

khrysalis table lamps

Used wine bottles, hand cut, polished, frosted and reassembled into works of functional art.

www.jerrykott.com

dawn hanging lamp

Dawn is an environmentally conscious lamp. She not only references nature in her sunny shape and color, she is also made from recycled mini blinds.

www.replayground.com

volivik

Classic chandeliers have always been large sparkling objects of fascination. This one differs only in that the sparkle comes from light dancing upon numerous used BiC roll pens.

millennium chandelier

Stuart Haygarth endeavours to give banal and overlooked objects a new significance. This chandelier is made of 1000 exploded party poppers collected on 01.01.00 after the millennium celebrations in London. Each popper is suspended on a line from a platform above. The sculptural shape sways and moves like an organic form when hit by a breeze of air.

www.stuarthaygarth.com

tide chandelier

The tide chandelier is created from clear and translucent objects – man made debris collected over time by Stuart Haygarth on an English beach. Each object is different in shape and form, yet they come together to produce one sphere. The sphere is an analogy for the moon, which affects the tide that in turn washes up the debris.

www.stuarthaygarth.com

parans

Parans is a solar lighting system that employs new technology to bring sunlight into buildings using fiber optic cables. It promises to deliver energy savings and provide a more natural environment for home or office, thereby promoting productivity and wellness.

ufo

The ufo light is made from an acrylic glass outer shell which houses optical fibers. These fibers efficiently transmit light from the power source to where it is needed (the end light point), but they only carry the light and not the electricity or the heat generated by the source. as such, they're ideal for illuminating wet places such as fish tanks and swimming pools. They're energy efficient because a single low energy source can be used to illuminate multiple end points.

www.neueslicht.de

fire & ice coffee table

Ecosmart makes environmentally friendly open fireplaces powered by denatured ethanol, which is a renewable energy form that burns clean and is virtually maintenance free. The fire and ice coffee table has the burner on one side and a recess for growing a little patch of grass (or perhaps to chill your champagne) on the other.

www.ecosmartfire.com

igloo

One of ecosmart's freestanding fireplaces powered by denatured ethanol. It is flueless and entirely portable. Take your energy efficient fireplace to any room in the house.

www.ecosmartfire.com

buddington bear rug

A humorous political and environmental comment on the practice of hunting. Using traditional hooking methods, this rug utilizes fabric scraps and cut-offs, salvaging unwanted materials.

www.loyalloot.com

persian rug

Cork is a natural, renewable resource, biodegradable and environmentally friendly. Trees are harvested by stripping them of their exterior bark every nine years with no harm done to the tree. The top layer of this "Persian" rug is made of cork, giving it a warm and natural feel. Its substrate layer of recycled tire rubber adds cushioning and durability. It's a natural and affordable flooring alternative to the area rug.

www.groupinc.com

little field of flowers

You'll feel as if you're resting in a cool meadow on a hot summer day – your own small place for relaxing and daydreaming on all natural wool.

www.nanimarquina.com

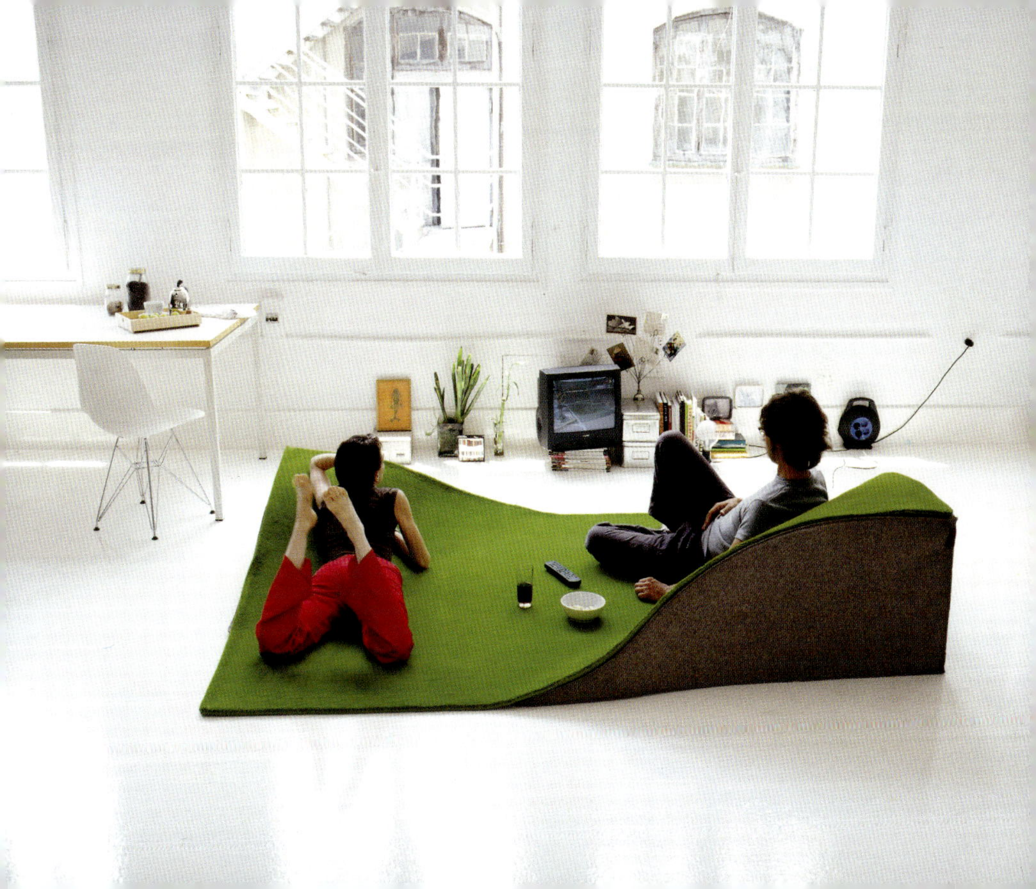

coral

Handmade organic cotton flannel pillow with wool felt appliqué.

www.balanced-design.com

light sleeper

Using electroluminescent technology that allows traditional textile surfaces to become a reactive light source, light sleeper is an illuminating personal alarm integrated into bedding that gently wakes in the most natural way.

www.loop.ph

organic cotton

Fine organic cotton sheets, which are eco-friendly and pure next to the skin, are complemented by a throw cushion screen printed on hemp linen.

www.looporganic.com

bamboo blanket

Bamboo comfort is a line of ultra-soft, 100% bamboo fiber bath towels, dish towels and blankets. Bamboo fiber textiles are extremely soft, antibacterial, and more absorbent than cotton, and they dry faster, too. Many textiles require chemical treatments to achieve these characteristics, but the oblong, hollow structure of bamboo fiber equips these towels with each trait naturally.

www.mad-mod.com

FURNITURE

chairs | tables | screens | shelving

oeuf crib

For the design and safety conscious parent this cot has a solid birch base, environmentally friendly MDF made of recovered wood fibers and a non-toxic white finish.

www.oeufnyc.com

green lullaby cradle

Instead of buying a heavy synthetic cradle for your newborn baby's first three months, try this one constructed entirely of cardboard. It's biodegradable and also collapses for easy transport.

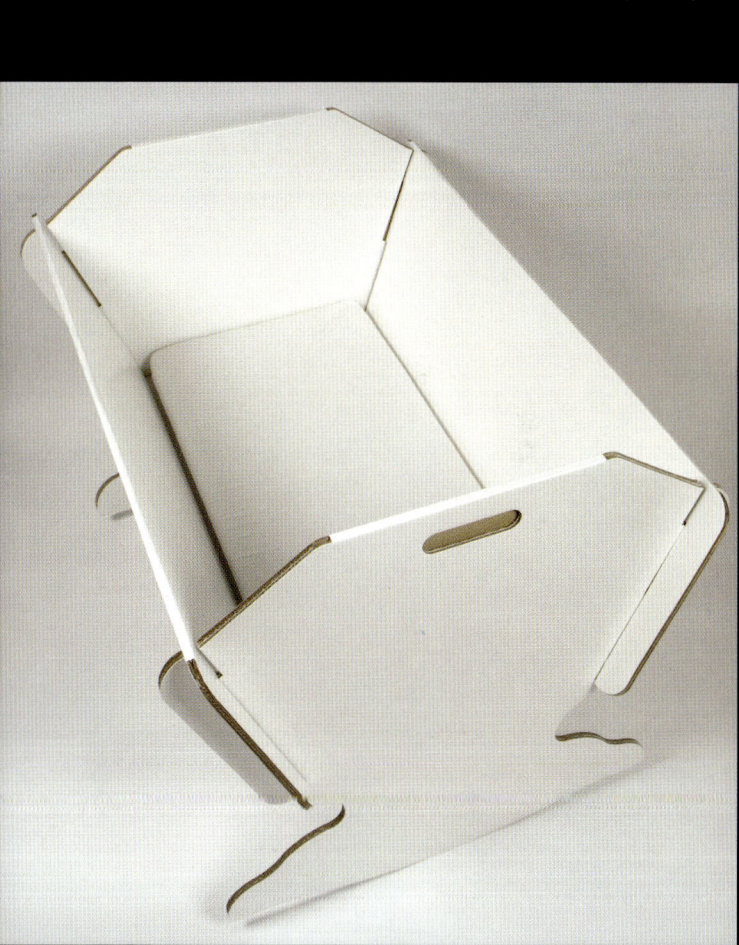

nest seat

A fun, soft and practical seat made from waste foam scaps covered in 100% organic cotton printed with low impact fiber-reactive dyes. Neco is also careful in selecting responsible manufacturing partners.

www.neco.com.au

kid's spring chair

A contemporary kid's rocking chair made from sunflower board and a truck spring.

www.cambiumstudio.com

RD4 chair

The "roughly drawn" chair is made from 100% recycled packaging waste (e.g. plastic food wrapping and milk bottles), and each chair is individually hand woven. Various shades of color arise from the blended packaging waste used in the process.

www.cohda.com

human nest

Bamboo is loved by environmentalists because it thrives without the use of fertilizer or pesticides and naturally improves the soil wherever it grows. This chair is constructed with a bamboo frame and scrap fabrics. Its design was inspired by the way birds build their environments.

www.emilypilloton.com

annie the shopping trolley chair

DOB: 2001. Previous life: shopping cart.

pallet chair

A groovy chair from a project called 10,TEN,X. The project consisted of 10 designers who had to make something for £10 from material sourced within 10 kilometers.

www.studiomama.com

blood chair

A striking plastic chair created by designer Sarah Blood from waste packaging using Codha's unique "URE" process (uncooled recycled extrude). By avoiding virgin plastic in their chairs, Cohda saves about 89 kilowatt hours in a standard 8kg/17lb blood chair. That's sufficient energy to run a 60-watt light bulb continually for 1,483 hours, or 2 months.

www.cohda.com

a la lata chair

The name A LA LATA, which literally means "to the can" in Spanish, comes from a Colombian phrase, which refers to doing things spontaneously, but with a lot of energy and enthusiasm. A la lata is constructed with 1,739 aluminium can tabs.

www.carlosmontana.com

vertibral

The vertebral is designed to move like a human spine and can be shaped into various bench styles or even used as shelving. Designer Joseph Keenan has produced it with renewable wood from managed forests. Eso group stands for "environmentally sustainable objects group".

seed bench

This seat is made from pressed sunflower seed husks, a rapidly renewable agricultural fiber product. The sawdust from production is given to a local dairy farmer to be used as bedding for cows.

www.stewdesignworkshop.com

bath and beyond

An old bath that was cut, bent and given legs in order to become a chair – with a surprisingly comfortable result.

www.reddishstudio.com

wooden chair

Made from recycled timber and lumbar destined only for firewood, a single block of European hardwood is transformed into a chair that now won't simply go up in smoke.

www.natanelgluska.com

www.johnhoushmand.com

exbox bench

The ex-box bench came about when designer Giles Miller was developing a cardboard bed for the homeless. It can be adapted to any desired length simply by slotting together a chosen amount of cardboard shapes.

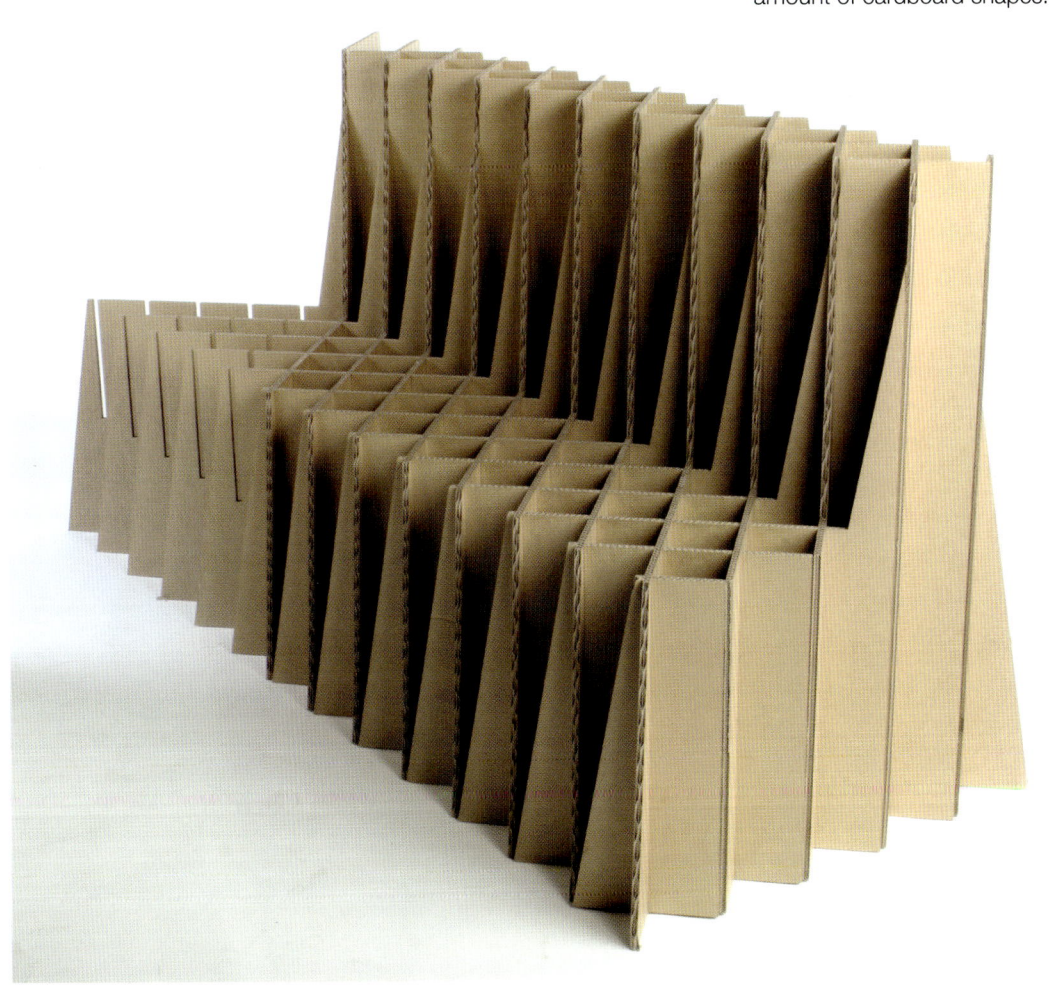

www.farmdesigns.co.uk

n+ew

A stool-sculpture-installation which freezes electronic waste in time with epoxy resin. The feet of the stool are made from melted recycled aluminium.

www.rodrigoalonso.cl

becca stool

These stools may look and feel light, but they're strong. Bamboo's tensile strength is 28,000 pounds per square inch, whereas steel is 23,000 pounds per square inch.

www.modernbamboo.com

sway stool

The cork used in this stool originates from the waste of the bottle stopper industry.

www.danielmichalik.com

hanging chair

Efficiently designed and cut from a single sheet of ply, this chair arrives flat and can be stored flat. Raw studio is as green as possible when they make furniture, because according to them, "it would be rude not to".

www.rawstudio.co.uk

pooktre

Pooktre is an emerging art form in harmony with the environment. With 20 years of research behind them, Peter and Becky Northey have mastered the art of shaping trees into functional art for the garden and home. Their latest plantings will produce living houses.

www.pooktre.com

cow benches

A series of unique hand-sculpted pieces each with a different name and shape. The benches serve as *memento mori* to remind us that we are mortal and our excesses are of fleeting value.

www.julialohmann.co.uk

dog bed

You can love your pet and the planet with this dog bed made from soft faux suede stuffed with recycled fleece scraps.

www.tailsbythelake.com

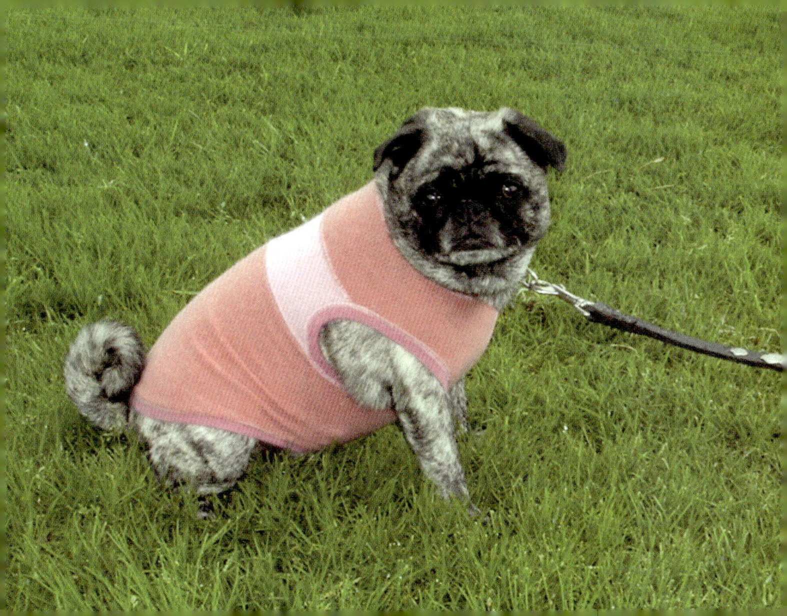

coffee table

A stylish table made from recycled coffee grounds rescued from coffee shops! the finish resembles a combination of stone, leather and chocolate.

www.rawstudio.co.uk

clamp-a-leg

The clamp-on legs are a more compact alternative to trestle tables. they come as an individual set of four legs and can be used with any surface. In this case a used door makes a perfect table top.

dining table

The Gore Design Co specializes in the design and creation of eco-friendly concrete countertop products and provides an alternative to the more commonly found granite and Corian products. Their concrete includes industrial by-products such as fly-ash, heavy metal free pigments and voc-free sealers.

www.goredesignco.com

erosion sink

The erosion sink poetically and beautifully reminds us of the fragility of the natural environment.

www.goredesignco.com

Reestore takes everyday waste objects and turns them into charming yet functional pieces of furniture and accessories, in this case a side table made from a re-used wash drum.

scrapile table

A beautiful table made from wooden off-cuts from Steinway & Sons, the Guggenheim Museum and a few local woodshops. Included in the mix is bio-composite cut-off (wheat board and dakota burl), bamboo, mahogany, walnut, poplar, maple, pine, spruce, oak and about 3 or 4 different types of plywoods.

www.scrapile.com

table of trash

A desk literally throwing itself into the waste basket!
It's made from "wellboard" which incorporates recycled
paper in its construction. The material is strong,
recyclable and very light, weighing just 4kg.

www.marielouise.se

"traffic" coffee table

A thin white board, unnoticed on a public pathway, gets trodden on, kicked at and cycled over. When retrieved, sealed with an eco emulsion and made into a table top, it provides a grubby snapshot of what city life entails.

www.ryanfrank.net

box table

Adding value to packaging. A cardboard box that converts into a useful table after it has exhausted its original role.

www.gonsherdesign.com

stop table

Dealing with traffic, graffiti artists and BB gun-toting youngsters day after day is a rough job, so stop signs of a certain age get taken out of circulation. Artist Tripp Gregson recruits the best-looking of these retirees and converts them into versatile tables.

www.uncommongoods.com

fenced in table

This piece re-purposes pre-cast iron fence pieces by cutting them up and welding them together into a table base.

www.uhurudesign.com

compacted table

A stunning coffee table created from compacted aluminium window frames.

www.trashformaciones.com

table #2

This bold design by Fredrikson Stallard brings the outdoors inside. Rough hewn sustainable birch is meticulously flattened and strapped together in an archaic method of creating a table without glue.

www.citizen-citizen.com

A stoolen is born every time Bill Hilgendorf collects enough hardwood scraps from local wood shops and an old bicycle rim to hold them together.

hung

This table's unique design removes the need for vessels to hold possessions. The inherent value of the design is meant to last a lifetime, ensuring that it retains a non-disposable presence and remains precious to its owner.

www.loyalloot.com

paper table

The Matt Gagnon Studio approaches design with an emphasis on movement and material exploration. This table is made from recycled magazines and newspapers and is designed to hold your current reading material.

www.mattstudio.com

cardboard flute screen

Farm Designs are a British design collective. Giles Miller designed this wall screen from recycled cardboard. It's just one of a series of cardboard designs created to show how diverse the possibilities are for recycled material.

www.farmdesigns.co.uk

refocus

Refocus is a room divider constructed out of over 1,000 old film canisters recovered from film processing stores. The canisters are strung together with elastic, giving the piece the flexibility to be rolled up when not in use and when shipped.

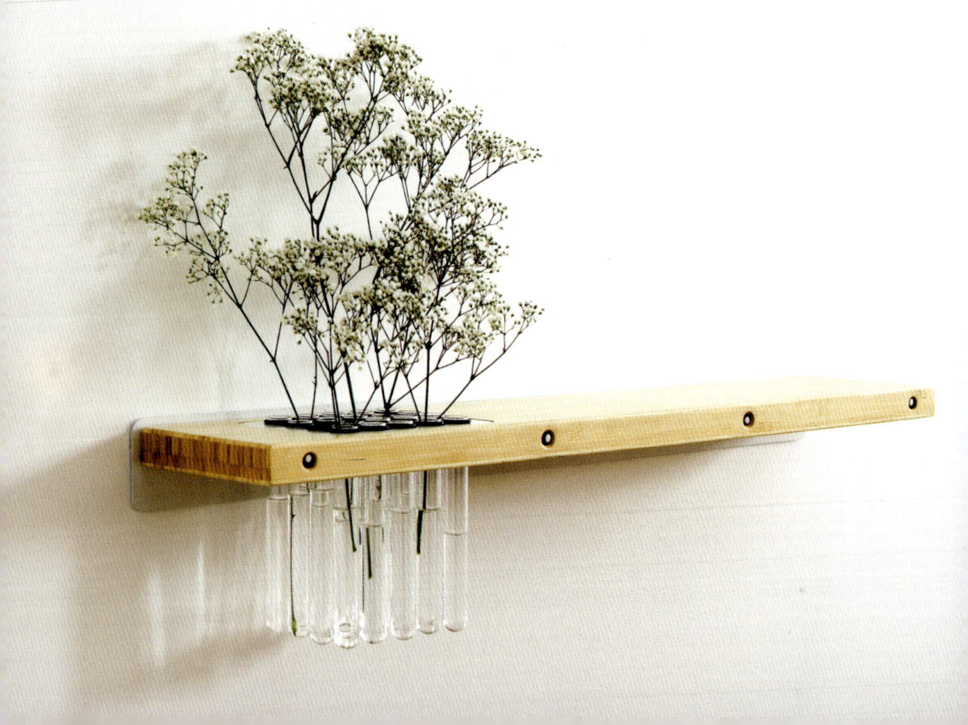

juxtaposed

For the first time, the world's most influential religious texts are brought together and presented on the same level, their coexistence acknowledged and celebrated. The juxtaposed shelf is made from reclaimed hardwood and is available in a limited edition of 50.

www.mikeandmaaike.com

books

Large old books of outdated titles have been assembled
with a specially designed metal connector to form
a wave-like modular book structure.

www.aisslinger.de

bamboo stagger

A modular multi-functional bamboo shelving unit that is durable and environmentally conscious.

www.bravespacedesign.com

the hackney shelf

Designer Ryan Frank set up white boards at various points around East London in order to attract the work of graffiti artists. He then took down the graffiti covered boards and transformed them into mobile shelving units, bringing street art into an interior environment. They're made from OSB board which contains waste woodchips compacted into a sheet material.

www.ryanfrank.com

full slant

Bamboo was chosen for this coffee table and shelving unit for its unique strength and beauty and to show that sustainable materials are more than mere material substitutes. Books can also expect to live a longer life when they are able to rest at an angle rather than tipping over all the time as they do on conventional shelves.

www.rhubarbdecor.com

OUTSIDE

environs | transport | afterlife

www.indoorlandscaping.de

loop biowall

A strong and flexible tension-compressed system that becomes a living wall that divides space and cleans the air we breathe.

www.loop.ph

vertical garden

Six molecules of water plus six molecules of carbon dioxide produce one molecule of sugar plus six molecules of oxygen – and that's the bit we want more of in our atmosphere. The vertical garden designs of Patrick Blanc are a stunning way to get more oxygen into our atmosphere.

A simple invention designed to turn brackish fresh water or salty sea water into safe drinking water, now being tested in Yemen by CARE.

prosolve 370

A decorative, three-dimensional architectural tile coated with titanium dioxide (Ti02), a pollution-fighting technology that is activated by ambient daylight. The tile reduces vehicular air pollution, including nitrous oxide and ground-level ozone.

www.elegantembellishments.net

rainwater tiles

Glazed earthenware paving set designed to divert rainwater and irrigate trees in urban areas.

www.promisedesign.info

e-v sunny bicycle

The first all-solar electric bicycle has solar panels built into the wheels which feed power into a 500-watt front hub motor. Speed along with the power of the sun.

www.therapyproducts.com

cycloc

Make your green machine a wall feature indoors or out with this secure bicycle storage solution, available in 100% recycled plastic.

www.cycloc.com

4000e electric scooter

Escape the clutches of the petrol pump and zip around town exhaust-free on this electric scooter. Its ingenious design focuses on minimizing the moving parts for easy maintenance so the only moving parts are the brakes, throttle and the wheels themselves.

www.neco.com.au

env

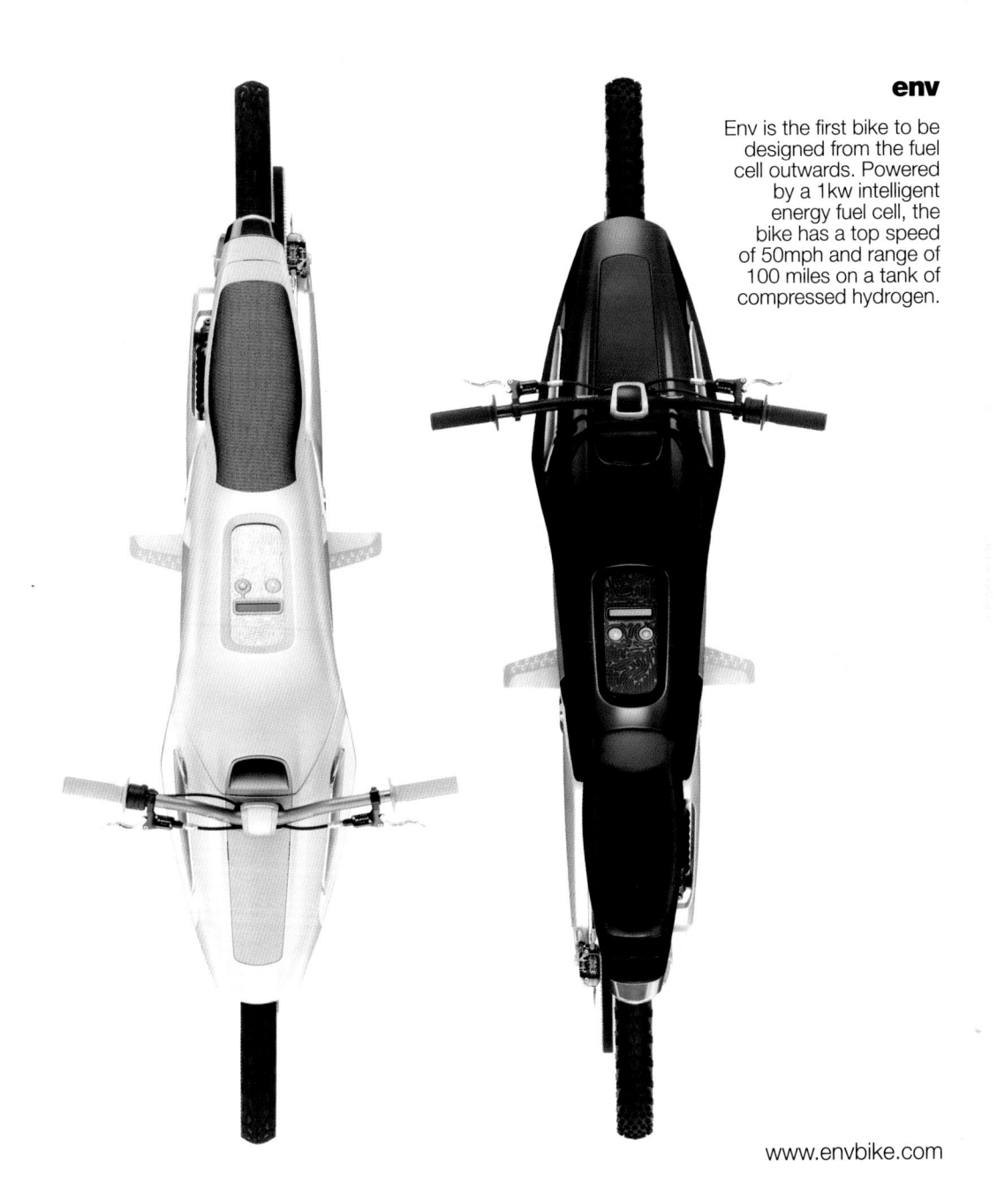

Env is the first bike to be designed from the fuel cell outwards. Powered by a 1kw intelligent energy fuel cell, the bike has a top speed of 50mph and range of 100 miles on a tank of compressed hydrogen.

www.envbike.com

astrolab

Venturi is a carbon neutral company and its cars represent 0 consumption and 0 emissions. Designed to facilitate inter-urban travel, the Astrolab has a top speed of 75 miles/hour and autonomy of 68 miles. with photovoltaic cells covered by a film of nanno-prisms enabling denser concentration of solar energy, the Astrolab is the first high-performance solar vehicle to be commercialised in the world. The Astrolab's design and performance evokes a racing yacht, advancing silently while making the best use of the elements provided by nature.

eclectic

The world's first commercially available energy autonomous vehicle. With a top speed of 30 miles/hour and autonomy of 31 miles, the Eclectic is intended to be driven in urban areas. Powered by solar panels and a wind turbine, the Eclectic can be supplemented, if necessary, by electrical recharging. The avant garde design, evocative of the Lunar Rover, gives priority to the photovoltaic cells which compose its translucid roof.

www.venturi.fr

sustain minihome

An elegant and modern yet autonomous home. The minihome is constructed from sustainable materials and offers off-the-grid living; heating, water, waste and power are all dealt with internally and no foundations are needed.

www.sustain.ca

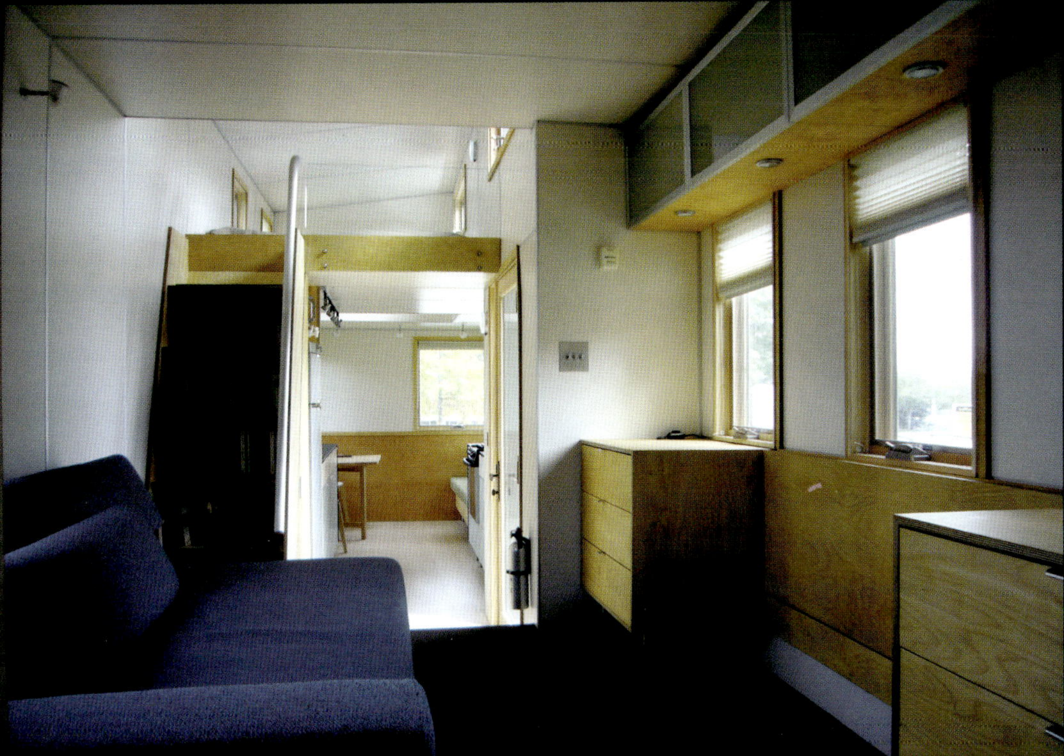

bird feeders

After a person is cremated they can opt to have their ashes mixed with bird food and applied to this bird feeder. The person is in a sense reincarnated through the life of the bird. Perhaps the ultimate in recycling?

www.nadinejarvis.com

rest in pieces

A ceramic urn that you hang above the place you wish to scatter the ashes. Holding the urn together is a degradable thread. Over time the thread falls apart causing the urn to drop. The urn smashes when it hits the ground scattering the ashes. The thread has a lifespan of 1 – 3 years, allowing an element of the unknown to enter into the process of when the person will actually be laid to rest.

www.nadinejarvis.com

ecopod

Research from The Natural Death Centre in London has shown that 89% of coffins used every year in the UK, that's some 600,000 coffins, are made from chipboard covered with laminate. Burning chipboard coffins pollutes the atmosphere, and burying them pollutes the earth. Ecopods are different. Made from naturally hardened 100% recycled paper, they are ideal for an eco-friendly, non-toxic burial in a green field site.

www.nigelsecostore.com

photo credits

Most of the designers who contributed images to this book did not request a photo credit. Those that did are listed below in order of appearance.

giggles bracelet | www.margauxlang.com | © Azad

button cuffs | www.tamsinhowells.com | © Dave Fowler

pinwheel vintage shoes | www.margaulange.com | © Azad

organic cotton sneaker | www.johnpatrickorganic.com | © Jan Galligan

amy dress | www.ciel.ltd.uk | © Ben Gold

UM | www.joshjakus.com | © Aya Brackett

wattson | www.diykyoto.com | © Toby Summerskill

eggflat | www.joshjakus.com | © Aya Brackett

flamp | www.guixe.com | © Imagekontainer

handlight | www.hubcapcreatures.com | © Drew Gardner

club chair | www.johnhoushmand.com | © davidjacquot.com

clamp-a-leg | www.jorrevanast.com | © Lucas Hardonk

books | www.aisslinger.de | © Steffen Jänicke